THE
MAJESTY OF
GOD
IN THE OLD
TESTAMENT

A Guide for
Preaching and Teaching

Walter C. Kaiser Jr.

Baker Academic

a division of Baker Publishing Group
Grand Rapids, Michigan

© 2007 by Walter C. Kaiser Jr.

Published by Baker Academic
a division of Baker Publishing Group
P.O. Box 6287, Grand Rapids, MI 49516-6287
www.bakeracademic.com

Printed in the United States of America

Library of Congress Cataloging-in-Publication Data
Kaiser, Walter C.
   The majesty of God in the Old Testament : a guide for preaching and teaching / Walter C. Kaiser, Jr.
     p. cm.
   Includes bibliographical references and indexes.
   ISBN 10: 0-8010-3244-X (pbk.)
   ISBN 978-0-8010-3244-8 (pbk.)
   1. God (Christianity)—Attributes. 2. God (Christianity)—Biblical teaching. 3. Bible. O.T.—Criticism, interpretation, etc. I. Title.
BT130.K35 2007
231′.4—dc22
                                         2006035279

For the members of
The Gordon-Conwell Theological Seminary
Leadership Team

1997–2006

Robert Landrebe
Barry Corey
Sidney Bradley
Alvin Padilla
Lita Schlueter
Bill Levin
Howard Freeman

"See what God has done!" (Num. 23:23)

Contents

INTRODUCTION

"You thought I was altogether like you." (Ps. 50:21b)

One of the greatest enhancements that could come to most evangelical teaching and preaching—indeed, the best preparation for a genuine revival and church renewal among the people of God worldwide—is a whole new appreciation for the majesty and greatness of our God as presented in the Scriptures. Unfortunately, one of the best sources for this teaching—the Old Testament—is all too often neglected in our teaching and preaching.

In this book, I wish to give God's people new insight into this avenue of thinking and believing by reviewing ten outstanding Old Testament texts that set forth the majesty of our Lord. Each chapter begins by exploring a key concept, an important term, an archaeological background, or a word study that will enhance our appreciation for the text under review and add to the depth of our study and teaching.

The center of our emphasis will be on the magnificence and majesty of our God. Our word *majesty*, of course, comes from the Latin root that means "greatness." To describe someone as majestic is to speak of that person's greatness and to offer our respect for who that person is. But the fact is that there is no one like our God; he is incomparably magnificent and awesome in all his person, works, and plans!

Alas, however, much of our teaching and preaching suffers from a mediocre view of God's majesty. We are too much like those chided in Psalm 50:21, who "thought [God] was altogether like [one of them]." As presenters of the Word of God, we desire to soar to the heights of the heavenlies and to lift the sights and hopes of our listeners to the very portals of the throne room of God himself; yet, more often than not, we feel frustrated and vacuous in the final results, both in our private study of the Word of God and in our listening habits on Sunday. Therefore, we, and the people we serve, starve for the awesomeness, greatness, and sheer majesty of the King of kings and Lord of lords.

In one of his letters to Erasmus, Martin Luther said, "Your thoughts of God are too human." So too today, the "god" of this twenty-first century often does not equal the majestic and awesome Lord of the Scriptures. Instead, the "god" all too frequently announced today is more an invention of our own thinking and sentimentality. There can be no stopping point halfway between the absolutely majestic God depicted in Scripture and no God at all. J. B. Phillips was on the mark some years ago when he published the aptly titled *Your God Is Too Small.*

John Piper came to a similar conclusion in his revised edition of *The Supremacy of God in Preaching.* He began his preface by declaring:

> People are starving for the greatness of God. But most of them would not give this diagnosis of their troubled lives. The majesty of God is an unknown cure. There are far more popular prescriptions on the market, but the benefit of any other remedy is brief and shallow. Preaching that does not have the aroma of God's greatness may entertain for a season, but it will not touch the hidden cry of the soul: "Show me thy glory."[1]

The psalmist did not let his heart starve for lack of expressing the majesty and greatness of God. Psalm 145:1–5 taught Israel (and now teaches us) to sing:

I will exalt you, my God the King;
    I will praise your name for ever and ever.
Every day I will praise you
    and extol your name for ever and ever.
Great is the LORD and most worthy of praise;
    his greatness no one can fathom.
One generation will commend your works to another;
    they will tell of your mighty acts.
They will speak of the glorious splendor of your majesty,
    and I will meditate on your wonderful works.

It was this same awesome majesty that Moses and the people of Israel sang about after successfully crossing the Red Sea. They hymned, "In the greatness of your majesty you threw down those who opposed you. You unleashed your burning anger; it consumed them like stubble" (Exod. 15:7). And Elihu declared to Job, "God comes in awesome majesty" (Job 37:22). It was at that very point that God himself took up the keynote that Elihu had just struck and set out for Job a mind-boggling display of his wisdom and power as exhibited in nature. If Job was so determined to preserve his own legitimacy before God, then God challenged him to step forward and show his own "glory and splendor," his prized "honor and majesty" (Job 40:10), to see if what he had was anything like the glory, splendor, honor, and majesty of God! This quieted Job very quickly, and should do the same for us should we ever presume to put ourselves in God's place.

That is why David also urged his generation to "declare [God's] glory among the nations, his marvelous deeds among all peoples. For great is the LORD and most worthy of praise. . . . Splendor and majesty are before him" (1 Chron. 16:24–25, 27).

The awesome distance described by David that separates the mighty Lord from all imitations of the same is enough to startle even the most insensitive of souls. Here is the Creator of the universe, the Potter who holds sway over all the clay! He is indeed the one and only Creator of all.

"In the beginning God. . . ." Doesn't that say it all? How else can we begin? To whom can we go if not to our magnificently majestic God who graciously made us and everything around us and who sustains us by the word of his mouth and by his mighty power (Ps. 33:6, 9)?

That is the conclusion that the fugitives from Egypt came to as the nation Israel was born in that awesome event of the opening up of the Red Sea. They sang:

> "Who among the gods is like you, O LORD?
> Who is like you—
>   majestic in holiness,
>   awesome in glory,
>   working wonders?" (Exod. 15:11)

It was no different when Israel was about to cross over the Jordan River. Moses pleaded with the Lord:

> "O Sovereign LORD, you have begun to show to your servant your greatness and your strong hand. For what God is there in heaven or on earth who can do the deeds and mighty works you do? Let me go over and see the good land beyond the Jordan." (Deut. 3:24–25)

Exactly so! There is no god anywhere in the universe that can compete with the Lord our God in his deeds, works, or person, for his greatness surpasses everything and every other being. There is nothing, and there is no one, who can compare to him even in the slightest way.

The Reformers, of course, regularly appealed to the doctrine of the majesty of God (known in its Latin form in that day as the *maiestas Dei*) to point to his utter divine transcendence over all human categories. It is simply impossible for a person to comprehend the divine majesty of the Godhead. Instead, one must fall down before him in worship and prayer, as Calvin advised. For the theologians of the Reformation, the majesty of God provided the guidelines and boundaries for setting forth the doctrine of God.[2]

For some, God's majesty was a way of summing up all the divine attributes of the eminence or perfections of the whole Godhead: Father, Son and Holy Spirit. It was the term that spoke of the unreachable and unsearchable heights to which the essence of who God is could best be described. His majesty also denoted his lordship over all things and his right to act freely in all that he does.

Divine majesty is closely connected with worship and prayer to God. His glory and majesty can be seen in the created world around us and in the unswerving manner in which God fulfills all the promises he has made; therefore our most appropriate response is to fall down before him in adoration and worship.

God's majesty is likewise the revelation of his person. The disclosure of the infinite excellence of his divine person is tantamount to seeing the "face of God" or to being exposed to a "light inaccessible."[3] The "glory of God" is just as strong a manifestation of his person and presence.

The surpassing excellence of the majesty of God is a staggering thought. How then shall we preach, teach, and meditate on this lofty theme with any degree of adequacy or approximation? The psalmist, I believe, can help us. According to the ancient heading of Psalm 63, David worshiped God when he was in the Desert of Judah. He marveled:

> O God, you are my God,
>   earnestly I seek you;
> my soul thirsts for you,
>   my body longs for you,
> in a dry and weary land
>   where there is no water.
> I have seen you in the sanctuary
>   and beheld your power and your glory.
> Because your love is better than life,
>   my lips will glorify you.
> I will praise you as long as I live,
>   and in your name I will lift up my hands.
> My soul will be satisfied as with the richest of foods;
>   with singing lips my mouth will praise you. (Ps. 63:1–5)

How can a heart hungry and starved for God be filled? It can be filled only by beholding all over again the greatness and the glory of God. The soul-satisfaction that comes from feasting on the person, power, love, and glory of God is better than any banquet of the richest foods. In fact, one can get his or her fill of food, but there can never come any sense of being overly full or stuffed from the satisfaction of meditating on the greatness of our God. There is not a worry or a concern about becoming overweight or overindulging when it comes to our soul's hunger for God. It is simply limitless!

What a caution this raises, then, about all trite comparisons or limitations that we would make equal to the powers and qualities of God's greatness! To which of all God's works would we like to offer some comparable duplications of our own devising? What nation's achievements would we suggest as a match to the mighty works of God?

Obviously, there is nothing comparable. That is why we must be taught, or teach ourselves all over again, the biblical texts that call us to magnify the majestic and awesome name of our God!

Method of Presenting These Teaching Passages

In order to appreciate the depths that the ten passages expounded in this book contain, for each passage I have elected to focus on one or two aspects of study that demonstrate the emphasis of each Old Testament text. Thus, for one I will do a word study, for another an archaeological and historical background study, or a study from systematic theology. These studies, though brief and limited in scope, are just enough to suggest areas for emphasis when the passage is taught to a Bible study group, Sunday school class, or a congregation.

However, I am also interested in helping others get over the psychological barrier that the Old Testament presents to too many readers of the Bible. Therefore, I have stressed a simple method for identifying the title or topic for each text by using the focal point, or big idea, of that passage. My contention is that the focal point is almost always found right in the text itself—perhaps in a verse(s) that plainly says where the author was going as he drove home the principle(s) for which that piece of revelation was given.

After the title or the subject of the lesson, personal study, or sermon has been identified in the focal point of a passage, it is time to use the famous six interrogatives (Who? What? Why? Where? When? and How?). I apply each of these interrogatives to the title or subject of our passage in order to see which of these six interrogatives the scriptural text best answers. Usually one of the interrogatives will fit better than the others.

That leads to a search for a homiletical key word, since we wish to present our biblical passage from a consistent standpoint—a feature of good speech construction. Indeed, that is what speechmaking or teaching is all about. The teacher takes the same stance for the whole study and adopts and then examines the biblical text from that same standpoint in each of the main sections or stages found in the biblical writer's thought. This homiletical key word is always a noun, for we want to *name* whatever it is we are talking about. That noun also must be a *plural* noun, for generally we are making several main points in our talk. Finally, the third feature of this key word is that it must be an *abstract* rather than a concrete noun. The reason for this rule is that we want to go beyond the times, culture, and setting in which the biblical text was written and share it with all of God's children worldwide. Only one noun of this type must be outlawed: *things*. A talk that begins with the words "There are three *things* I want to say about this Scripture" does not tell us very much, for the key homiletical word is still missing as far as the three rules above are concerned: it fails to name specifically what is central in the passage.

With these few observations, we are ready to look at some of the grandest Old Testament texts on the greatness of our God. Join in the fun as we look at some old and some new friends in these texts. Before we proceed, however, we must consider a few possible objections that may arise from study and teaching on the magnificence and majesty of God.

Must Every Christian Lesson or Sermon Focus on Christ?

My friend Bryan Chapell, in his fine book *Christ-Centered Preaching*,[4] has argued that [all?] preaching is really about getting Jesus across to an audience as a worldview. If Christ is not preached, Chapell writes, it may be seriously questioned whether what we have heard is a Christian sermon or lesson. Chapell's thesis agrees with a similar thought in the writings of another friend, Sidney Greidanus.[5] Both Chapell and Greidanus allow that this does not mean that every verse or passage directly reveals Jesus Christ, but they do argue that every passage in the Bible has as its larger context the person, work, and necessity of Christ. In like manner, Calvin Miller wants to know this about every sermon: "Is the sermon about Christ?"[6]

So how shall we respond if the following ten messages focus in their entirety on God the Father and not specifically on God the Son? Bryan Chapell does admit that there are thousands of passages that contain no direct reference to Christ. If that is so, then how is the teacher or preacher to remain Christ-centered in these texts that are silent on his person and work?

Chapell replies that when neither the scriptural text nor scriptural typology presents us with the Savior, the teacher or pastor must rely on the greater context of the Bible in order to bring out the redemptive focus of that message.[7] Usually this is done by appealing to the progressive nature of biblical revelation as it comes to full flower in the New Testament. But this is neither the theocentric method of teaching and preaching advocated by John Calvin nor the christological method used by Luther. Instead, it is a redemptive-historical-christocentric method of preaching that views the "whole counsel of God" in light of Jesus Christ.[8] Greidanus correctly noted that it is improper to read Christ back into the Old Testament, for that would be eisegesis, or reading meanings from the New Testament into the Old Testament text. That, of course, is the real issue that presents itself here, and that calls for great caution. So how does Greidanus propose to remedy this situation? He would have us "look for legitimate ways of preaching Christ from the Old Testament in the context of the New."[9] But what has happened to expository preaching in that case? It appears to begin with the text of the Old Testament, but it appears to rely on the New Testament for the real solid stuff, that is, the theology and principles we can apply directly to our lives. Even if this is not what is intended, this is what often results in the hands of many Christian teachers and preachers.

But how can we do such jumping from the Old Testament text to the New Testament without committing the methodological *faux pas* of eisegesis? Greidanus's solution is that we must never take "an Old

Testament text in isolation, but [we] must always understand [read: exegete?] the text in the contexts of the whole Bible and redemptive history."[10] Simply to take an Old Testament text and preach on it is to preach an Old Testament sermon, Greidanus warns. Of course, that aphorism is nothing more than a tautology: Old Testament texts yield Old Testament sermons! But who said that was bad or undesirable—as if someone other than God were the source and author of the Old Testament or that these texts had such temporality written over them that almost all of them were now passé and useful only as primers or sermon starters? And if that is true, then what of those audiences to whom these Old Testament messages were first preached who did not have a New Testament in the back of their Bibles?

What exactly is meant when we use the phrase "Old Testament sermon?" Do we simply mean a sermon that is derived entirely from the Old Testament? Or do we mean a sermon that was formerly valid but is no longer *kosher* for believers in the post-Old Testament era? How could those who lived in the Old Testament era have done any less, or any more, than to limit their teaching and preaching to what revelation was available up to that time? It is not as if the revelation did not come from God or that it was of some inferior quality, was it? Or did those Old Testament saints get it wrong?

What makes a sermon a *Christian* sermon or lesson? Must all sermons and lessons based on the Old Testament move inexorably on to the New Testament if they wish to earn a "Christian sermon rating" (CSR)?

But the discussion grows even more complicated. Greidanus boldly claims that redemptive-historical preaching does not ask, "What was the author's intended meaning for his original hearers? but, how does the redemptive-historical context from creation to new creation inform the contemporary significance of this text?"[11] In that same context, Greidanus favorably quotes Christopher Wright: "We may legitimately see in the event, or in the record of it, additional levels of significance in the light of the end of the story—i.e., in the light of Christ."[12] But notice that Wright carefully uses the word "significance." Greidanus, however, goes on to affirm dangerously "that a passage understood in the contexts of the whole Bible and redemptive history may reveal *more meaning* than its author intended originally."[13] Such a view of the plurality of meanings that exceeds the truth-intentions or assertions of the original authors who stood in the counsel of God ultimately runs the risk of forfeiting the divine authority that is to be found in the passage; this view could be taken to imply that the human author wrote his text in a purely automatic and mechanical way, as if it were dictated or whispered word for word in his ear without the human author having a proper idea of its messianic or future redemptive meaning. But if the meaning God intended exceeds the meaning the human authors recorded, where shall we locate this additional surplus meaning? If it is not in the grammar and syntax, it must be somewhere between the lines! But if it is between the lines, whatever else it is, it is not *written*. And if it is not written, is it inspired? The apostle Paul makes it clear that only the *graphe*, what is written, is inspired (2 Tim. 3:15–17). Now we are really in a jam!

All too often the depth that many search for as contemporary believers, and the depth that God intended his human writers of Scripture to get—and which they did get, for they recorded it in the text—is missed in our day. As a result, too frequently we feel we must run to the New Testament as quickly as possible to enhance what some wrongly regard as the minimalistic Old Testament meaning with a super-spiritual meaning infused from the New Testament, thus adding Christian values to an otherwise "Judaistic sermon" to help the church or those in our modern world. But how wrong such judgments and procedures would be!

This is not to say that, after the meaning and message of the Old Testament has been established on its own terms, we must act as if the New Testament were not available at all. The New Testament really does exist, and we can (and must) often use it in our *summaries* to our major points and/or to the whole message, pointing out how the beginning, middle, and end of the unified plan and message of God in the total Bible fits so nicely with what also is taught in the Old Testament text. I have argued elsewhere for the unity of the "promise-plan" of God that encompasses the whole Bible and therefore shows one divine mind, one plan, and one story of salvation in all sixty-six books.[14] It is against this backdrop of viewing the grand plan and story of the Bible that I find agreement with my friends Chapell, Greidanus, and Miller. But I must not *prematurely* infuse New Testament values and meanings back into the Old Testament in order to sanctify it before I independently establish, on purely Old Testament grounds, the legitimate meaning of the Old Testament text. If I perform such an infusion, I only pretend that I am accurately giving the word of God exactly as he wanted it taught and preached from that Old Testament passage. So let us first do our work of true exegesis on the Old Testament text. Then, having gotten the meaning God revealed at that point in time, let us see how our Lord developed that same word, if there is further development, on into the rest of the Bible.

Must Every Sermon Chiefly Be "Interesting"?

According to the "New Homiletic,"[15] every sermon or lesson from the Bible must chiefly be "interesting." But what biblical support could we give for this assertion? This is not to make a case for boring or ineffective lessons and sermons, of course. But we must ask who determines or supplies the criteria whereby we can say that a sermon has "interest."

The apostle Peter concluded that some of Paul's writings were hard to understand (2 Pet. 3:16); would such difficult matters pass the "interest" test? Why didn't Peter just create his own meanings and not worry about what propositional teachings Paul might have had in mind? If teaching and preaching also have as one of their main goals to effect change in the lives of the listeners, would all of those apostolic or Old Testament prophetic calls for change be welcomed at first blush as being "interesting" by all listeners?

In fact, the criteria of "interest" may be linked to more modern values, such as the brevity of the message or the number of memorable illustrations peppered throughout its short duration. This matter of "interest" also may indicate that our contemporaries are becoming more like connoisseurs of listening to messages rather than being those who are moved in their hearts to act and become doers of the word (James 1:22).

Rather than making "interest" the key test for a good sermon, we would suggest as an alternative the double tests of: (1) does the lesson or sermon accurately reflect what is being taught by the author of the text? and (2) has that text been applied to our modern and contemporary contexts of living and acting so that I am called to change for the glory of God? These two lodestars will guide us as we set forth the magnificence and majesty of our God in the following ten passages.

Is the Best Use of the Old Testament Merely as "Illustrative" of the New?

Some evangelical ministers and teachers will cheerfully confess that they rarely preach a message from the Old Testament; instead, they preach from the New Testament and use the Old Testament merely for illustrations of the truths or points they are trying to make from the later testament. They feel that in this manner they are indeed preaching the whole "counsel of God" (Acts 20:27 KJV).

Haddon Robinson comments that this approach to "preaching from the Old Testament" is deficient in two ways.

> First, homiletically it ignores the basic principle of illustration: we illustrate the unknown from the known. If an illustration has to be explained, don't use it. Because most passages of the Old Testament have to be explained in detail to a modern audience, using Old Testament stories as illustrations takes unfamiliar incidents in the Old Testament to explain or apply unclear texts in the New. More important, however, reducing the Old Testament to an anthology of illustrations for sermons based on the Gospels or Epistles slights the Old Testament authors who were theologians in their own right. . . . [C]ertainly they did not write to provide illustrations for other biblical writers.[16]

As we conclude this chapter, may the deep desire of those who teach and preach God's Word, whether for their own personal Bible study or for a group large or small, be that the blessed truth of all of God's Word would be shared openly and joyfully to the building up of the whole body of Christ.

Remember, it was the apostle Paul who reminded Timothy—who had access at that time only to the first thirty-nine books of the Bible (i.e., the Old Testament)—that "all Scripture is . . . profitable" (2 Tim. 3:16 KJV). Not only could the Old Testament be God's instrument through which individuals could be saved ("the Holy Scriptures, which are able to make you wise for salvation through faith in Christ Jesus," v. 15), but those same texts also could bring "teaching, rebuking, correcting and training in righteousness, so that the man of God may be thoroughly equipped for every good work" (vv. 16–17).[17] The first of these five purposes for teaching and preaching the Old Testament is certainly salvific and christological, but the other four still stand as legitimate goals. It is in this light, then, that we dare to announce with great boldness and fervor the teaching of the Old Testament on the supremacy and majesty of our incomparably great God, who exceeds every boundary and limitation known to any and all mortals and who alone is God of gods, King of kings, and Lord of lords.

1

Magnifying the Incomparability of Our God

Isaiah 40:9–31

Introduction

Every passage that has been chosen as a text for teaching and preaching from the Old Testament in this book can be enhanced by the teacher or preacher if some of the special studies that probe its depths of meaning are carried out in connection with its use in the classroom, pulpit, or private study. In Isaiah 40:9–31, the repeated emphasis on the fact that God cannot be compared to any person or thing gives us one of the greatest teaching texts in the Bible on the incomparability of God in his person and his acts.

Such teaching passages (sometimes called "chair passages," or in the Latin, *sedes doctrine*)[1] are excellent opportunities to focus on key aspects of the theological and doctrinal teaching of the Scriptures. Therefore, in preparation for preaching on this passage, we will pause to examine the centrality, significance, and importance of this teaching in the Old Testament. Fortunately, we are helped

by a seminal study from some years ago that will stand for a long
time to come.

A Special Study: On the Incomparability of God

In 1966, E. J. Brill published a landmark book by C. J. Labuschagne
entitled *The Incomparability of Yahweh in the Old Testament*. In a
most remarkable way, it highlighted those qualities of our God that
set him apart from all pretenders and claimants to the name of our
God. It also emphasized those attributes of God that are most char-
acteristic and fundamental in describing and affirming who he is.
Moreover, it drew attention to God's uniqueness and singularity in a
polytheistic world. Over and over again, the cry went up from those
who had met this Lord that he is beyond comparison, just as those
on Mount Carmel did during the days of Elijah, when they cried,
"The LORD—he is God! The LORD—he is God!" (1 Kings 18:39).
No one could be compared with God, and no one was on his level
in any way at all!

Labuschagne studied the various ways in which God's incomparability is expressed. First, there is the *negative expression*: "There is
none. . . ." A good example of this is 1 Samuel 2:2.

> "There is no one holy like the LORD;
>   there is no one besides you:
>   there is no Rock like our God."

In Exodus 9:14, this same type of negation is used as the Lord declares
that he will send the ten plagues on Egypt and Pharaoh "so that you
may know that there is no one like me in all the earth." The same
affirmation, set in a similar formula, can be found in Deuteronomy
33:26; 2 Samuel 7:22; 1 Chronicles 17:20; 1 Kings 8:23; Psalm 86:8;
and Jeremiah 10:6, 7. Modifications of this formula can be found
in Deuteronomy 32:31; 2 Chronicles 14:11; 20:6; Isaiah 46:9; and
Jeremiah 10:16. Though the truth is stated in negative terms, the fact
remains that God is in a class by himself with no competitors.

A second formula uses the *rhetorical question*, "Who is like . . . ?"
The Lord himself asks this question in Isaiah 44:7 ("Who then is like

me?") and in Jeremiah 49:19 ("Who is like me?"). This same question appears in the meaning of a number of names such as Micah, Michael, Mishael, Micaiah, and the like. In these names the interrogative "Who?" is the Hebrew particle *mî*, and the "as" or "like" is the Hebrew particle represented in English as *c*, *ch*, or *sh* followed by the divine name taking the form of *El*, or *[Y]ah*. Seven psalms and ancient songs of Israel use this same rhetorical question. They are: Psalm 35:10 ("Who is like you, O LORD?"); 71:19 ("Who, O God, is like you?"); 77:13 ("What God is so great as our God?"); 89:8 ("O LORD God Almighty, who is like you?"); 113:5 ("Who is like the LORD our God?"); Exodus 15:11 ("Who among the gods is like you, O LORD?"); and Micah 7:18 ("Who is a God like you?"). In addition to these hymns and songs, we also find Elihu saying in Job 36:22, "Who is a teacher like [our God]?" And Moses asks in Deuteronomy, "What other nation is so great as to have their gods near them the way the LORD our God is near us whenever we pray to him?" (Deut. 4:7) and "For what god is in heaven or on earth who can do the deeds and mighty works you do?" (Deut. 3:24). Note that the comparison is not between the gods of the other nations and Yahweh, but between Israel, who has such a great God as her Lord, and the other nations! These are the greatest questions a mortal could ask. But the answer to each one leads to the realization that nothing, indeed no one, compares to the living God revealed both in the Old Testament Scriptures and later on in our Lord Jesus Christ.

A third way of expressing such incomparability is found in *other rhetorical questions* besides the one that asks "Who is like . . . ?" The reason for this is that the Old Testament delights in using rhetorical questions to designate absolute power, distinctiveness, and outstanding uniqueness. One form of such a question stresses the humbler position of the one asking it in comparison to the Lord himself. For example, Solomon declared in 2 Chronicles 2:6, "But who is able to build a temple for him, since the heavens, even the highest heavens, cannot contain him?" Likewise, David had offered the same humble judgment as he, too, contemplated building the house for God in 2 Samuel 7:18: "Who am I, O sovereign LORD, and what is my family, that you have brought me this far?" David repeated the same sentiment as he gathered the materials to ready the building of the temple that Solomon would take up on his father's behalf. He decried in 1 Chronicles 29:14, "But who am I, and who are my people, that we should be able to give as generously as this?" Something of the same sentiment underlies Psalm 8:4: "What is man that you are mindful of him?" (cf. Ps. 144:3; Job 7:17; 15:14; 40:4). Even when this formula is expressed contemptuously from the mouths of mockers, it still shows how exalted God is beyond all other comparisons. For example, Job disrespectfully inquires, "Who is the Almighty, that we should serve him?" (Job 21:15). Job would shortly find out who this incomparably great God is, and he would quickly shut his mouth and remain silent before God. In the same way Pharaoh would learn a similar lesson after he mockingly asked, "Who is the LORD [Yahweh], that I should obey him and let Israel go?" (Exod. 5:2). No different was the king of Assyria's commander, who blurted out, "Who of all the gods of these countries has been able to save his land from me? How then can the LORD [Yahweh] deliver Jerusalem from my hand?" (Isa. 36:20; cf. 2 Chron. 32:14). But Moses knew the answer, for in his song in Deuteronomy 32:39 he recorded God's announcement, "See now that I myself am He! There is no god besides me."

Another form of a *rhetorical question expects the answer, "None."* The expected answer to all comparisons of incomparable acts by our Lord is: "None but Yahweh alone!" Thus Isaiah asks five questions in Isaiah 40:12 as to who compares to God in his power over nature. There are none who can compare! And in verses 13 and 14 he asks five more questions to see if there are any rivals to God in his wisdom and understanding. Again, there are none (cf. also Deut. 3:24; Prov. 30:4; Job 34:13; 36:23; Eccles. 8:1b). This type of question is exhibited in a large number of passages in the Old Testament. These questions may point to God's unrivaled actions in the past or to deeds that only he can perform (cf. Exod. 4:11; Lam. 3:37).

One more way this type of question can be asked is, *"What does x have in common with y?"* Thus Jeremiah inquires, "For what has straw to do with grain? . . . Is not my [God's] word like fire . . . and like a hammer that breaks a rock in pieces?" (Jer. 23:28–29).

Finally, the writers of the Old Testament used *verbs to denote possible similarity or equality.* For example, the verb meaning to "be in a row," "be on a line with," or "be equal with," in Psalm 40:5 is best translated, "none can equal you," or "no one can be on a level with you." Likewise, Psalm 89:6 says, "For who in the skies can equal Yahweh?" or who "can be on a level with Yahweh?" Again, in Isaiah 40:18, the prophet asks, "To whom, then, will you compare God? What likeness will you put on a level with him?" And in Isaiah 40:25, the question is still worth asking: "To whom [then] will you compare me, that I should be like him?" (cf. Isa. 46:5; Ps. 89:6).

It is clear that nothing stands on a par with or in any way rivals or challenges the magnificence and magnitude of the God whom the prophet Isaiah presents in 40:9–31.

Now let us apply this collection of expressions of unrivaled magnificence as background understanding or appreciation to the study of our first passage.

An Exposition of Isaiah 40:9–31

The best place to start when preparing to teach or preach on a passage is to locate the focal point, or what Haddon Robinson calls the "big idea" of the passage. Invariably, this will be found in a key verse, phrase, or (in a narrative portion) an epitomizing speech or quotation from the lips of one of the speakers in the story. In this prophetic speech passage, the prophet uses the rhetorical question in verses 18 and 25 to ask, "To whom, then, will you compare God?" and "To whom will you compare me?" It is always from the focal point that we are able to derive the topic or subject title for our lesson or sermon. Here it will be: "Magnifying the Incomparability of Our God."

We note that the literary form of this text is poetical verse rather than prose. For English readers, this also can be seen from the way the English text is set in indented form in many versions. We will not pause here to set out for inspection all the characteristics of Hebrew poetry, but certainly the reader can detect a different feeling as he or she reads this text as opposed to the preceeding chapter of Isaiah.

In this poetical form, we note that there are three distinctive strophes. Verses 18 and 25, with the repeated rhetorical questions we just noted, easily mark the second and third strophes (which may be thought of as poetic paragraphs). These questions act as headings, or to use the technical term, rubrics, for what follows. In Egypt, headings in a similar type of work would have been inked in red, hence our current term *rubric*, which is derived from the Latin word for *red*. The first strophe is not as easily identified, but if verses 9–11 act as an introduction to what follows, giving the topics to be covered, then verses 12–17 would appear to form the first strophe.

Now that we have determined that there are three strophes that carry out the focus or big idea of this passage (which unusually in this case also double as the rubrics in vv. 18 and 25), we must ask how the writer unfolded his thesis or focus. One of the best ways to determine the answer to this question is to ask which of the six interrogatives best fits this text: Who? What? Why? Where? When? or How?

After trying all six of these interrogatives, I find that "What?" fits best. True, the text also asks "To whom?" will you compare God, but more is raised here than competing persons. One is being asked to match up multiple topics and situations to the magnificence of the one true living God!

Now I need a homiletical key word that names the element common to each of the strophes. This word must be a noun, for we are going to name something. It will also be a plural noun, for there usually is more than one paragraph, strophe, or scene in a teaching or preaching pericope (i.e., a block of text, in which all the verses deal with the same idea). Not only must this key word be a plural noun, but it also must be an abstract noun. Since we are going to try to formulate principles, it would not be helpful to use a concrete noun. That would land us in an ancient context rather than teaching for our own day, describing only what was said and not allowing us to apply it to the present needs of our hearers. Therefore, we have settled on the homiletical key word of "areas." Thus, our proposition is: "What are the areas that show magnificently that our God is incomparable?" And there are three such areas set forth in the three strophes. Now we are ready to introduce the line of discourse in this text.

Few things stir one's attention and pique one's interest as do the words "Ladies and Gentlemen: The President of the United States!" followed by the Marine Band playing "Hail to the Chief." But that is exactly how our passage begins its introduction in verse 9: "Behold your God!" (You will have to imagine the music, for that is found in the poetic structure.) All who bring the good news of the gospel to Zion and Jerusalem are to get up on a high mountain and raise their voices to their loudest pitch with the jubilant presentation: "Hear ye, hear ye! Behold our God! Take one more long, steady look at him in all his magnificence and splendor, for he exceeds all comparisons and any known or unknown rivals."

The theme is further introduced in verses 10–11, just as some musical pieces set forth their themes in an opening overture. There is the area of his *power*, for our God will come with power as his "arm" rules for him. Then there is the area of his *personhood*, for he is alive and he brings his reward and recompense with him. Surely he sees and knows what has been going on in the time prior to his coming. That is because he is a real, living person who has witnessed all that has happened. The last area announced in verses 10–11 is his *pastoral care*. He is the good shepherd who knows how to treat lambs and hurting ones with gentleness.

The resulting outline will be:

Focal Point: vv. 18a, 24a—"To whom, then, will you compare God?"
Homiletical Key Word: Areas
Interrogative: What? (are the areas that show the magnificence of our incomparable God?) Our God is incomparably great:

I. In His Power (Isa. 40:12–17)
   A. Compared to Nature (v. 12)
   B. Compared to Individuals' Wisdom (vv. 13–14)
   C. Compared to Nations (v. 15)
   D. Compared to Our Models of God's Greatness (vv. 16–17)
II. In His Person (Isa. 40:18–24)
   A. Compared to Dead Idols (vv. 18–20)
   B. Compared to Princes and Nobles (vv. 21–24)

III. In His Pastoral Care (Isa. 40:25–31)
    A. Compared to Finite Things (vv. 25–26)
    B. Compared to Despondent Ones (vv. 27–28)
    C. Compared to the Strength of Youths and Draftees (vv. 29–31)

I. Our God Is Incomparably Great in His Power (Isa. 40:12–17)

What can rival God's power or produce any sort of challenge that he could not easily overcome and supersede? Ancient Israelites, like modern inhabitants of the global village, must lift their sights and vision, for it is not simply that our God has been the Creator in the past; no, he is the present Regulator of the heavens and all the earth. That is why God's infinite power is exactly what we need for our present comfort and guidance. In fact, were this power of God more deeply seated in our thinking, we would not be so alarmed and disturbed by all the calamities, terrorists, and drug cartels that appear to be ruling and reigning at the present time.

Compared to Nature. Isaiah posed five questions related to the power and omnipotence of God. He proposed five measuring devices and five items to be measured in order to help us think approximately on the high order of the God who is presently ruling and reigning over all heaven and all earth.

The Measuring Devices:	The Items Measured:
The hollow of his hand	the seven seas
A man's hand span	the entire heavens
One-third of a bushel	all the dirt of the earth
A scale for weighing	all the mountains of the world
A double scale	all the hills of the world

Three-fourths of the earth's surface is comprised of the seven oceans, and yet all that could be held in the hollow of God's hand? Really? Yes, in comparison—if we are thinking on the high order of the God of Scripture! Alternatively, think of the vastness of space and all the planets. Is this hugeness reducible to merely the distance from a man's thumb to his small finger? Yes; according to the Hebrew word picture used here and in comparison to the magnificence of the living God, all that space is insignificant. And can all the dirt and soil of the earth be reduced to just a third-of-a-bushel basket? Yes, if we compare that with the greatness of our God! And can all the mountains and hills of the world be dropped onto a steelyard scale, including a mountain almost six miles high named Mount Everest, and God still have no trouble balancing it and all others on the other side of this double scale? That's correct; that is, if we are thinking of God's power correctly and biblically. He is an awesome God, to say the least.

Oh, if this power of God were only more deeply impressed on our souls! What a difference it would make as we faced all sorts of tests, alarming crises, and the vicissitudes of life!

Compared to Individuals' Wisdom. But what if we were speaking not just about the power of God? Can we say with equal confidence that what we have ascribed to the power of God also can be said of his wisdom? After all, we have some very powerful computers and some extremely smart individuals on this earth. Will the brilliance of mortals rival in any way that possessed by our God and his omniscience?

Isaiah asks five more questions to help us get our thinking where it needs to be if we are even to begin approximating the God who is beyond comparison. The five questions are:

Has anyone understood God's mind?

Has anyone instructed or counseled him?

Has anyone enlightened the Lord on any matter?

Has anyone taught the Lord the proper way to go?

Has anyone taught him knowledge, or did he go to any of our schools?

What was ascribed to God's power and goodness in the previous section is now attributed to his wisdom and understanding. Just as the heavens, with all of their space, amounted only to the span of a mortal's hand in verse 12, so the same Hebrew word (*tikken*) is used to mean "to regulate" the mind of God in verse 13. In fact, the apostle Paul quotes verse 13 in Romans 11:34 to deter us from rash, brazen inquiry into the wisdom of God: "Who has known the mind of the Lord? Or who has been his counselor?"

Compared to Nations. But some will protest, "We know that God is all powerful and all wise. But what we worry about are the rogue nations of our present era. Some of them are stupid and would do anything to get their own way." Isaiah gives three similes in verse 15 to show us that all the nations' powers are but a drop in the bucket and like dust on the scales, if not just fine dust! In this manner the greatness of God is not brought forth in an abstract or detached way but in a way that allows us to see that in comparison to our Lord there is nothing that should even come close to worrying us. So, let us not exalt nations or any of their rulers, especially at the expense of diminishing the power, wisdom, goodness, and knowledge of God.

Compared to Our Models of God's Greatness. At this point we want to shout, "I understand. My view of God is so big, really! Let me show you by making a model of the enormity of my feeling for the incomparability of God. Suppose I take all the fabled cedar trees of Lebanon (comparable to the redwood forests of California) and all the cattle of that same country (comparable, say, to all the long-horned cattle of Texas) and make an offering to the Lord that is fifty miles long and seventy-five miles wide and twenty miles high, with thousands of the choicest cattle on top of it as a burnt offering! Will that not be a model worthy of showing, in a scaled-down version, how amazing this God is?"

Isaiah has to decline such a model, for it does not even begin to approach the order or magnitude of what we are talking about here. Verse 16 says such a model is "not sufficient!" It is plainly inadequate despite the use and number of such valuable trees and the quantity and size of the animals. Accordingly, he once again summarizes in verse 17 that the nations in all their prestige, power, influence, and resources are "as nothing"; indeed, "less than nothing," when compared to our God.

II. Our God Is Incomparably Great in His Person (Isa. 40:18–24)

Despite all the progress made thus far, Isaiah presses on to demonstrate that God is more than just a doctrine, an idea, or even "the force"; he is a living person. What are we going to put up as an adequate comparison to God? To what image will we compare him? (v. 18). Will any of God's rivals, past, present, or future, please stand up and show how they plan to meet such competition?

Compared to Dead Idols. Modern readers of this text might wish to pass over all teaching on idolatry, believing that this indeed is not our cup of tea. But it is! The essence of idolatry is making some person, place, or thing equal to or superior to the Lord. It could be our ideas, our goals, our programs, our children or grandchildren, or our institutions, but it still is a form of idolatry, even though we may not bow down to a form made out of wood, metal, or ceramic molding called Baal, Asherah, or Anat. Has not Paul told us that evil desires and greed are "idolatry" (Col. 3:5)?

True, idols are made to appear as if they have value and worth, for a wood- or metalworker shapes them, and then a goldsmith coats them with gold, and silver jewelry is placed on them. For those who are too poor to make such lavish gods, Isaiah has lots of fun offering advice. First of all, one should choose wood that will not rot. It would be devastating to have your deity come down with the rot or termites; it's just plain embarrassing! Oh yes, please get a craftsman who is skilled; some could not make a god if their lives depended on it! One thing more: nail that baby down! To come into your place for devotions in the morning to find your god dashed to pieces on the floor, as did the Philistines at Ashdod (1 Sam. 5), is really disturbing, especially if you did not bring Elmer's Glue to the worship services of your idol! Surely what one needs in an idol, or in any homemade god, is stability. So nail that idol down firmly and securely.

But God is not made of wood, metal, or any such thing; he is a real, living person. Idols are created by those who reject the living God and go in for imitations and replacements. But there just isn't any match, no matter how one tries to rearrange the facts. True, public opinion has great force, and often what pleases the masses passes for the truth. But such "truth" will eventually come crashing down of its own weight.

Compared to Princes and Nobles. So we must be asked once again: "Do [we] not know? Have [we] not heard? Has it not been told [to us] from the beginning? Have [we] not understood since the earth was founded?" (v. 21). What is it that we have missed so badly? Just this: God is now enthroned in heaven, ruling over all the masses of humanity. It is he who created all the universe, and it is he who now is guiding this world in accordance with the plan he has in mind (v. 22).

What shall we say for all the dictators, presidents, prime ministers, rulers, and generals currently in charge of things—even to the disruption of the work of the kingdom of God? We will say, according to this text, that God can and does remove princes and rulers of this world so fast that we hardly get to know them. No sooner do they appear than they are swept away into the dustbins of history by this omnipotent God. Thus, royalty and nobility are not exempt from the common lot. To think otherwise is to forget that our God cannot be placed on a par with any of the great leaders this world has or will yet ever see. God's authority and reality, as a person who exceeds the whole lot of all of these rulers combined, cannot be challenged or denied; he is absolute Lord!

III. Our God Is Incomparably Great in His Pastoral Care (Isa. 40:25–31)

Compared to Finite Things. We wonder if all we have seen of God so far, with all his power and all his unexcelled personhood, is too high and too transcendent for mortals such as we are. Yet, the final area explored in this passage is the area of God's pastoral care. Despite his magnificent transcendence, he is not so high and exalted that he cannot feel for us and shepherd us—even in our limited nitty-gritty history and geography.

So the prophet asks us once again, Do we still want to compare God to something besides himself? It seems the prophet lingers too long on this question, especially since there are no obscurities. Nevertheless, it is still necessary to repeat the question over and over again, for you and I tend to be more intimidated and terrified by all the empty masks of our time than we are strengthened by all the promises of the eternal God. We are so bombarded with saying after saying, commercial after commercial, and stories of terror and horror that we forget the eternal verities of the faith. So what do we say? Will we offer any comparisons, theoretically or practically, to the Lord himself?

Compared to Despondent Ones. In this vein, then, the prophet takes up the cause of all despondent persons who, like Jacob and Israel, say, "My condition, my cause, and my case is disregarded by my God." But why would we be so skeptical and despondent about the promises of God? This is inexcusable. Even if we have not said this out loud, we feel that our personal pain is just too heavy for the Lord.

What did we think? Did we suddenly think that God is not eternal? Did we think he might have become wearied and exhausted from doing good? (v. 28). God has not fainted (from any neglect of taking food), nor has he diminished in his capacity to take on work. Instead, his grace is all we need. What is true of our Lord is applied by Paul in 2 Corinthians 12:9 to all believers. God knows, according to infallible criteria, when he should interpose his help and strength.

Compared to the Strength of Youths and Draftees. In fact, just when we grow weary and weak, he supplies out of his fullness the power and strength we need. Why, even the youth and the young men in the prime of life and health stumble and fall all over the place out of exhaustion and weakness. But not this Lord. All true strength comes from him. The power of God comes to its peak thrust just when we are at our weakest point.

So let us put all our trust and solid confidence ("hope") in the Lord, for that is how men and women, boys and girls, soar like eagles. They take off and fly. In fact, they keep on going, running and walking. Why? Because their help is in the Lord, who cannot be compared in one iota to anyone or anything else! Great is our incomparable God!

So let us say to the cities of the world: "Hey, listen up all of you inhabitants: take one more steady, long look at our God, for behold he comes with all might, wisdom, and power. Instead of puffing up ourselves, our success, our churches, our institutions, our children, or our intelligence, we must exalt the Lord almighty to whom no one compares or even comes close." Let us sing with the hymn writer and Paul's benediction in 1 Timothy 1:17:

Immortal, invisible, God only wise,
In light, inaccessible hid from our eyes,
Most blessed, most glorious, the Ancient of Days,
Almighty, victorious, Thy great name we praise.

(Walter C. Smith, "Immortal, Invisible, God Only Wise")

Conclusions

1. Why, then, should believers be so frightened and intimidated by all the empty challenges of our day if our Lord is beyond challenge and beyond comparison in his power, person, and pastoral care?
2. Name whatever we might think would be an issue, a problem, a relationship, or a situation that is unsolvable, and this teaching regarding our incomparably great God takes precedence over every competing force we could rally to the cause.
3. But more is called for than a mere cognitive recognition of God's greatness and incomparability; we need to invest our lives, our resources, our children and grandchildren in one of earth's most strategic contests.
4. If our God is a most secure winner on all fronts, why are we so hesitant to commit ourselves and all that we have to him and to his cause? Our proper response is to lay at his feet all that we are and have for the magnification of his name, honor, and success.

2

MAGNIFYING THE GREATNESS OF OUR GOD

DANIEL 4:1–37

Introduction

Two topics call for some special engagement prior to our looking into the text of Daniel 4: (1) What is meant by the "greatness of God?" and (2) Who is this monarch Nebuchadnezzar, and why does Holy Scripture give this pagan ruler a full chapter in the Bible to describe an experience he had?

First, the matter of "greatness" must be treated in order to give us a better background for teaching or preaching this text. In fact, five times (4:3, 11, 20, 22, 30 [= 3:33; 4:8, 17, 19, 27 in Hebrew Bible]) this chapter focuses on the Aramaic word for "great" (*teqef*, "grow strong"). This chapter speaks of the tree in Nebuchadnezzar's dream becoming "large/great and strong" (vv. 11, 20 [8, 17]). In Scripture, the tree is often used as a symbol of the ruler, as Pharaoh was so signified in Ezekiel 31:1–9 (also cf. Ezek. 17:22–24; 19:10; Amos 2:9; Isa. 6:13; 11:1). And as Daniel interprets the dream for this monarch, he declares, "You have become great and strong" (v. 22 [19]). But Nebuchadnezzar still did not "get it," for twelve months later he strutted out onto the roof of his famous palace and boasted, "Is this not the great Babylon I have built as the royal residence, by my mighty [the noun *teqef*] power and for the glory of my majesty?" (v. 30 [27]).

So where does greatness lie? Is it in mortals, their dominions, building feats, and achievements? Not at all! For it was this monarch himself who celebrated the greatness of God's "signs," "wonders," and works and declared openly at the end of his seven-year ordeal, "How great are [God's] signs, how mighty his wonders" (v. 3).

One of the first places we can see the greatness of our God is in his mighty acts/miracles (Ps. 145:3, 6). These works of God cover all that he has done from the creation of the world to such landmark acts as effecting the exodus of Israel from Egypt. But even more significantly, that same greatness of God can be seen in his "mighty act" of giving the covenantal promise to David in 2 Samuel 7:21. That act of greatness included giving to David, and the whole messianic line that followed him, a dynasty, a kingdom, and a throne that would endure forever (2 Sam. 7:16). God's greatness also could be seen in the way he cleared out the Canaanites ahead of Israel as they came to occupy the land (2 Sam. 7:23).

But above all of God's works, it is his very "name" that shows us that only God is great! (Josh. 7:9; 1 Sam. 12:22; 1 Kings 8:42; 2 Chron. 6:32; Ps. 76:1; 99:3; 145:3, 6; Jer. 10:6; 44:26; Ezek. 36:23; Mal. 1:11). God's "name" is more than merely the vocable by which he is called; it stands for his character, his reputation (Exod. 3:15), his doctrine (Ps. 22:22; John 17:6), his ethics (Mic. 4:5), and his attributes (Ps. 139).

The last words the Islamic jihadists uttered as they crashed the hijacked American and United Airlines planes into the World Trade Center towers in New York City, the Pentagon outside Washington, D.C., and a field in Pennsylvania on September 11, 2001, was "*Allah akbar*," "God is great." But if only they had known the God and Father of our Lord Jesus Christ and his greatness! All else would have gained its proper perspective. Yes, only God is great, and no one will compare to his greatness in his person, works, or power.

But what of that king in Babylon who conquered all the ancient Near East and thought he was so great? Is there any comparison to the living God and his greatness? Let us take a brief look at the achievements of Nebuchadnezzar and see if he measures up in any way to our God.

Few monarchs in history have reached the heights of power and glory that King Nebuchadnezzar (605–562 BC) of Babylon attained. And far fewer have achieved the remarkable building success that he demonstrated in reconstructing ancient Babylon. No wonder he boasted as he did in Daniel 4:30!

We are dependent in part on the Greek historian Herodotus,[1] who wrote a century and a half after Nebuchadnezzar's day, for a description of this amazing achievement. Babylon was a marvel of urban planning, for the city was a somewhat squeezed rectangle, itself laid out in rectangles with some very wide streets named after the gods of Babylon. A bridge connected the eastern, or new, city with the western city across the Euphrates River, as its course flowed in those days. Stone piers on each side of the river were some six hundred feet apart and anchored in six boat-shaped pillars of baked bricks set in bitumen. A thirty-foot-wide footpath made of wooden planks spanned the river, but according to Herodotus, the planks were taken up each night so the inhabitants of either side of the river could not slip across and steal from the other during the night. The houses in the city varied in size from sixty by sixty feet up to one hundred and thirty by one hundred and thirty feet. They were usually one story high with flat roofs and had between eight and twenty-six rooms in each house.

The city could be entered through any one of eight gates, the most famous of which was the northern Ishtar Gate, rising to nearly forty-seven feet high. This gate featured magnificently colored lapis lazuli glazed bricks and other bricks in yellow relief depicting alternately a bull (a symbol of the god Adad) and a dragon (symbolizing the god Marduk). These motifs repeated along the whole face of the wall.

Robert Koldewey, who excavated Babylon from 1899 to 1918, was able to demonstrate how security conscious Nebuchadnezzar was. Koldewey found that the city was protected on the east by an outer wall (variously estimated from 11 miles long to Herodotus's 480 stadia, or 55¼ miles). The city was surrounded by a series of walls that provided the most formidable barrier to invaders yet devised by a monarch. Two massive walls enclosed the rectangular city. The inner-most measured twenty-one feet thick and the outermost measured eleven feet thick. Thus, if the outer wall was breached, the invader would find himself trapped between these two walls. Moreover, every sixty to sixty-five feet the walls were topped by watchtowers, three hundred sixty in all, reaching ninety feet high at least, but probably not three hundred feet high as mentioned by Herodotus. The walls were wide enough to accommodate several chariots riding side by side. In front of the outer wall there was also a water-filled ditch or moat-like system that hindered direct attacks on the city.

The Ishtar Gate opened up onto the one thousand-meter-long Processional Way, which was 73½ feet wide, paved with imported stone, and called *Aibur-Shabu* (meaning "the enemy shall never pass"). This road led in a straight line north and south through the city. Along this processional street, bordered by high walls deco-rated with a series of one hundred twenty lions (symbols of the goddess Ishtar) in enameled relief on glazed bricks and spaced at sixty-four-foot intervals down the road, were another five hundred seventy-five dragons or bulls (symbols of the gods Marduk or Bel) evenly interspaced as well. The most famous staged tower, or zig-gurat, along Processional Way was the *E-temen-anki*, "the House of the Foundation of Heaven and Earth," which rose three hundred feet high and probably could have been seen for miles around the city in this flat terrain. Some have estimated that 58 million sun-baked clay bricks (many of which were stamped with Nebuchadnezzar's name or dedicatory messages) were used to construct this seven-staged tower. It was named *Esagila* and dedicated to Marduk, the city's patron god. A temple stood on top of the tower and was reached by any one of the three staircases leading up to it. This was probably the much-talked-about ziggurat (temple tower) of Babylon. There were some fifty other temples inside the city limits, with the grand temple of Marduk at the end of Processional Way.

Just inside the Ishtar Gate along Processional Way was Nebu-chadnezzar's palace, made of yellow bricks, with floors of white and mottled sandstone. Probably in this palace were the famed "Hanging Gardens," considered to be one of the seven wonders of the ancient world. Some believed the gardens were built for Nebuchadnezzar's wife, who was said to have missed the mountains of her homeland up north in Media. Situated on the west side of the palace was a massive walled fortress.

Babylon was a marvel of architectural planning and construction. It was the greatest city of the world in its day. The accomplishments represented there were indeed staggering and spectacular for their times. The empire had reached its zenith, not only on the battlefield, but also in its cultural and architectural achievements.

Appreciation of some of these archaeological details will prepare us to gain some background for the boastful claims of this monarch, who wanted to challenge the greatness of all rivals—including, as it turned out, the greatness of God! Let us now go to Daniel 4 and learn how God's greatness surpasses all substitutes or cheap imitations such as those proffered by Nebuchadnezzar.

An Exposition of Daniel 4:1–37

The focus of this chapter is repeated in identical terms in Daniel 4:17, 25, and 32—"The Most High is sovereign over the kingdoms of men and gives them to anyone he wishes." Coming from the mouth of a monarch who had achieved so much on the battlefield and in building such a magnificent city as Babylon, surely this is a testimony to the fact that this man had finally learned his lesson—one he thought all the rest of us also should learn lest we should fall into the same trap he did. In fact, he began his testimonial of his bitter experience with words that are very similar (Dan. 4:3b) to those of the psalmist in Psalm 145:13: "Your kingdom is an everlasting kingdom, and your dominion endures through all generations." That is where greatness could be found. Clearly, the subject of our teaching and preaching is going to be about the greatness and sovereignty of our God and his kingdom!

Now we can look at how this chapter breaks down and how the scenes of this narrative portion carry out the theme—the focal point of the chapter, or the big idea of this text—found in verses 17, 25, and 32. There are four divisions, determined by the number of narrative scenes as indicated by a change in location, setting, speaker, or time. Scene 1 is verses 1–3, which contains a retrospective look over the event to be narrated and a poetical device called inclusion. Then in scene 2, verses 4–18, we are told of a dream that happened in Nebuchadnezzar's palace. This is followed by scene 3, Daniel's interpretation of that dream in verses 19–33, also in the palace, but at a later time. Finally, in scene 4, at the end of the seven years of personal hardship for this monarch, we find Nebuchadnezzar restored to his throne and former position and speaking again in verses 34–37.

Our subject for our teaching or preaching will be "Magnifying the Greatness and Sovereignty of Our God." The interrogative we will use is "What?" And the homiletical key word will be "areas." What, then, are the areas where the greatness of our God can be raised up for all to see and praise our majestically wonderful Lord?

   I. Our God Is Great in His Works (Dan. 4:1–3)
   II. Our God Is Great in His Warnings (Dan. 4:4–18)
   III. Our God Is Great in His Wrath (Dan. 4:19–33)
   IV. Our God Is Great in All His Ways (Dan. 4:34–37)

It is now time to introduce the lesson or sermon. Is it not true that the air is filled with exclamations of greatness these days? The weather is great! My team is doing a great job! My cornflakes taste great! The economy is great! And so it goes.

That is how the king of France, Louis XIV, felt. He preferred to be known not as Louis XIV, but as "Louis the Great." He died in AD 1717, but he had previously arranged for his coffin to be brought into the great cathedral of Notre Dame. He wanted all candles to be extinguished except the one on top of his coffin. To mark this occasion, he had asked that the court preacher, Massillon, give the funeral oration. As Massillon mounted the stairs to the high pulpit, it seemed as if all was not right, so he descended the stairs and blew out the remaining candle over Louis's casket, only to remount the pulpit and announce twice in French, "Only God is great! Only God is great!" Louis XIV was dead. Yes, he is remembered today, but mainly through Louis XIV furniture.

In Daniel 4, King Nebuchadnezzar also must learn this lesson the hard way. He will be put out to pasture (literally) and sustain

himself on "grass" (the original kind of grass) as he is afflicted with
the disease we today refer to as boanthropy, "ox-man" disease. No
wonder this chapter ends with his advice to all who followed him to
avoid pride and not fall into the trap he had fallen into: "Those who
walk in pride [God] is able to humble" (Dan. 4:37c). God did just
that for Nebuchadnezzar. He humbled one of the greatest empire
builders of antiquity!

I. Our God Is Great in His Works (Dan. 4:1–3)

It almost sounds like a truism: the greatness of our Lord can be
seen in all his works (Dan. 4:1–3). It is all that and more. The prophet
Daniel must have been somewhere around forty-five or fifty years
old as Nebuchadnezzar was coming to the end of his long reign
(605–562 BC). Some surmise that this event might have taken place
around 570 BC. If so, then two years prior to this, Nebuchadnezzar
had ended his long siege of the coastal city of Tyre (Ezek. 29:17–18).
But despite his frustrations over not being able to conquer Tyre,
God had rewarded him with the gift of the land of Egypt, just as the
prophet Jeremiah had predicted (Jer. 43:10; 44:29–30). A fragmentary
archaeological tablet noted that "In the 37th year [which began April
23, 568 BC], Nebuchadnezzar, king of Babylon, marched against
Egypt to deliver battle."[2]

But at the pinnacle of the king's success, a warning came from
God; Nebuchadnezzar chose to disregard it for twelve months (Dan.
4:29). That led to seven years of living off the land and existing more
like an animal than a human being.

It was in light of this that Nebuchadnezzar wrote "to the peoples,
nations and men of every language, who live in all the world" (v. 1).
He had some advice for all those living on earth at that time, advice
we ignore today at our own peril as well. He had seen the miraculous
working and spectacular deeds of the Most High God, for they had
been performed in his own life.

Talk about "greatness," said this quieted monarch who had had it
all, let me tell you instead about "how great are [God's] signs, how
mighty his wonders" (v. 3). Thus, a chapter appears in the Bible from
a pagan monarch under the permission of the Spirit of God, with

advice in verses 3b and 34b that acts as the framing text (or an inclusion) for the whole story: "[God's] kingdom is an eternal kingdom; his dominion endures from generation to generation."

Exactly so! Our Lord's greatness can be seen through his works. And lest we forget, remember how dramatically we too have seen the workings of our God in our recent history. From the fall of the Bastille on July 14, 1789, to the fall of the Berlin Wall in late 1989, God intervened so suddenly and so forcefully that we hardly had time to recall Western civilization's two-hundred-year love affair with humanistic values that had been substituted for divine values. It all came crashing down in a moment of time. Also gone in 1989 was a great world power, as the Soviet Union broke up, and Eastern Europe realized that the education it had treasured from the universities in the West had been declared spiritually and morally bankrupt and moribund compared with what it was now experiencing at the hands of a new Eastern Europe. Yes, God is still great in all his works!

II. Our God Is Great in His Warnings (Dan. 4:4–18)

But God is also great in all his warnings. Here begins the sad story of a king who had everything except the living God. Nebuchadnezzar tells us he was at rest in his palace and all was well in that enormous empire except for one thing: he had had a dream! That is not too bad for one who bore the burdens of state for an empire that covered everything from present-day Iraq to present-day Syria, Turkey, Israel, and all the way down the Nile River in Egypt! Only a disturbing dream—that is all? Many a monarch would love to have Nebuchadnezzar's problems!

Once again, the king resorted to his unusually incompetent batch of worldly advisers, the same quacks who had been unproductive in interpreting his dream in Daniel 2. But this dream "terrified" (v. 5) him. Of what he was so frightened, he did not know. Now the enchanters, soothsayers, magicians, and Chaldeans had rule books for interpreting dreams, so why didn't they give it a try? We do not know. All of them were on state scholarships, just like Daniel and his three friends Shadrach, Meshach, and Abednego (Dan. 3:12), who had been taken into captivity from the land of Israel as young boys in 605 BC. Finally, Daniel was called (v. 8). He (along with the other Judaic captives named above) had been given a Babylonian name (Belteshazzar) and was now "chief of the magicians" (v. 9).

Nebuchadnezzar expressed his confidence in Daniel and then went on to relate his dream. It went this way: "While lying in my bed . . . before me stood a tree in the middle of the land. Its height was enormous" (v. 10). Nebuchadnezzar went on to describe this tree in great hyperbole: "Its top touched the sky; it was visible to the ends of the earth" (v. 11). So what was the big deal? It was a tree with unprecedented height and a trunk of massive bulk with leaves healthy, beautiful, and possessing abundant fruit. Remarkably, all the beasts of the field dwelt under this tree, the birds roosted in it, and every creature was being properly fed. That was quite a tribute to a government stretched out over so vast a surface of the earth! All seemed fine. Why was he so terrified?

A "messenger" (v. 13 [10]), or "watcher," from God, a "holy one," descended from heaven and declared in alarming terms that the tree was to be cut down, its leaves stripped, its branches lopped off, and its fruit scattered. This "messenger" or "watcher" was probably an angel, as the term is rendered in the Greek Septuagint translation of this passage. The Aramaic word for "watcher," *'ir*, is found only here in Daniel 4 and in the pseudepigraphal writings of Enoch, Jubilees, and the Testament of the Twelve Patriarchs. Now angels are not effeminate creatures with an impossible number of wings as they are often depicted; they are God's messengers, who perform his bidding and carry out his will and plan. As God's lieutenants, they restrain the work of the prince of the power of the air, Satan, and they are often assigned to definite posts such as the prince of Greece or the prince of Persia. Even so, they are curious and very desirous of looking into the plan of redemption that God has provided for the people of God, as Peter affirms in 1 Peter 1:12.

It is important to note that in the middle of the declaration by the angel there is a significant change in the English version from neuter pronouns in verses 14–15a to masculine singular pronouns in verses 15b–16 (from "its, . . . its, . . . its, . . ." to: "him, . . . him, . . . his, . . . him . . ."). This is much like the significant shift in the prophecy against Tyre in Ezekiel 26:1–12 (where after predicting "many na-

tions" [v. 3] would come against Tyre, the text switches to talking
only about Nebuchadnezzar as the antecedent of "He . . . his . . . he
. . . his," until we come to verse 12, which suddenly has "they." At this
point it depicts a scraping of the mainland city and throwing it into
the sea to build a causeway out to the isle city of Tyre, one-half mile
out—which is exactly what Alexander the Great did three hundred
years after Nebuchadnezzar). In Daniel this change of pronouns signals that the tree is figurative and the message is aimed at a man, or as
it turns out, against Nebuchadnezzar himself. It is in this context that
the theme of the passage is repeated again in verse 17. God is doing
this "so that the living may know [personally] that the Most High is
sovereign over the kingdoms of men and gives them to anyone he
wishes and sets over them the lowliest of men." And so it has been
both before Nebuchadnezzar and after his time! Promotions do not
come from the east or the west, but from God—all of them, even
of those who lead ungodly nations and people! And Nebuchadnezzar urged (in effect), "Listen up all you who are living: greatness in
not found in mortals, their nations, institutions, or achievements,
whether they are intellectual, scientific, moral, or spiritual. Greatness
belongs exclusively and uniquely to our God. Period!"

III. Our God Is Great in His Wrath (Dan. 4:19–33)

God's greatness, sovereignty, and lordship may still be upheld
by many in terms of doctrine, but in practice these characteristics
tend to be diminished as soon as they are connected to God's holiness. We esteem and appreciate the greatness of God so long as it
is connected to his mercy, kindness, and love, but when exclusive
loyalty is demanded, a gentle disaffection can be seen, even among
the faithful. That is what is difficult about the greatness of God as
depicted in this third scene. The events happened in this way.

For a time the dream related to Daniel by the king "greatly per-
plexed" Daniel and "his thoughts alarmed him" (v. 19). Had the
dream been aimed instead at the king's enemies, it would have been
easier for Daniel to interpret it for the king, but alas, he said, "You,
O king, are that tree!" (v. 22). There was the nub of the whole matter. With great integrity, Daniel, like the prophet Nathan pointing

his finger at King David and saying, "You are the man!" does not waste any words or time in getting to the truth and the heart of the matter. Daniel told the king that, like the tree in the dream, "You have become great and strong," for "your greatness has grown until it reaches the sky, and your dominion extends to distant parts of the earth" (v. 22). But now you will be cut down just as the tree was, continued Daniel, leaving only a stump in the ground. You will be drenched with the dew of heaven and live like a wild animal for seven years until you finally come to acknowledge that "the Most High is sovereign over the kingdoms of men and gives them to anyone he wishes" (v. 25).

So there it is: God is able to bring cocky, proud, boastful, self-filled persons down off their high horses by reminding them that he (not they) is in charge. If we doubt that this is so, then ask King Nebuchadnezzar—or ask Mikhail Gorbachev, Boris Yeltsin, and Saddam Hussein.

Good preacher that Daniel was, he pressed home his appeal for a change of heart in this monarch before it was too late: "Therefore, O king, be pleased to accept my advice: Renounce your sins by doing what is right, and your wickedness by being kind to the oppressed. It may be that then your prosperity will continue" (v. 27). God wanted to see evidence of an inward change, as shown by the way Nebuchadnezzar left off his wickedness, stopped all oppression of the harassed, and acted in kindness toward the afflicted.

Some incorrectly teach, based on v. 27, that our sins can be atoned for by doing good deeds and giving alms to the poor. However, notice that the "doing what is right" and "being kind to the oppressed" are evidence of faith already possessed. The word that the NIV translates as "renounce" comes from the Aramaic word *peruq*, "to tear away" or "to break off," just as Aaron instructed the Israelites "to tear off" their earrings (they must have been clip-on earrings!) so that he could build the golden calf (Exod. 32:2). The Greek Septuagint and the Latin Vulgate mistranslated Daniel 4:27 [24], taking the word from another Aramaic root, *pdy*, similar to the Hebrew root *padah*, "to redeem," or as some want it, "to atone," but that value does not appear until post-biblical times, and it does not fit this context either. The New American Bible (NAB) translation (1970) rendered this verse: "Therefore O king, take my advice; atone for your sins by good deeds, and for your misdeeds by kindness to the poor; then your prosperity will be long." This Roman Catholic translation has a footnote on this verse that says, "A classic Scriptural text for the efficacy of good works." However, none of these translations will work in the context of the passage except as a call for a dramatic breaking with our sins in full repentance and the production of evidences that a change has come in the heart as witnessed by the way we now live.

IV. Our God Is Great in All His Ways (Dan. 4:34-37)

Twelve months passed, and the king still had not bought into the advice given by Daniel, even though he apparently had accepted the interpretation of his dream. To the contrary, he boasted as he walked on the roof of the famous palace, "Is not this the great Babylon I have built as the royal residence, by my mighty power and for the glory of my majesty?" (v. 30). While the words were still on his lips, God took away his royal authority, and he was literally put out to pasture on grass for the next seven years.

Seven excruciating years for Nebuchadnezzar passed, and finally he lifted up his eyes toward heaven. God restored his sanity (v. 34), and immediately he began to praise the Most High. In three active participles (praise, exalt, and glorify, v. 37), he gave continuous anthems of thanksgiving and praise to God. And he knew why God had done this as well: it was "because everything he does is right" and because "all his ways are just" (v. 37). Nebuchadnezzar had found out what too few find out or too many find out too late: "Those who walk in pride [God] is able to humble" (v. 37). The essence of pride is to take to oneself honors that rightly belong to another. This king, like the prodigal son, had to "come to his senses" (Luke 15:17).

Yes, God's dominion is everlasting and his kingdom will go on and on, unlike all mortal kingdoms. In comparison to God, all the peoples of the earth are simply nothings. God did what he wanted to do in the past, and he will continue to do as he pleases in the present and the future. Nothing and no one will stop him and say, "What are you doing?" (vv. 34-35).

Was Nebuchadnezzar truly converted? Calvin, Keil, and others say, "No." He failed to recognize God's grace and mercy in his daily praise, and so he still did not get it all straight. There is no record that he changed in the rest of his reign. But what he learned was so important that our Lord had him give his testimony in Scripture. So, pride does go before destruction and a haughty spirit before a fall (Prov. 16:18). Moreover, it is indeed a person's pride that brings each one low, but to one who has a lowly spirit, that one gains honor (Prov. 29:23). On the way to gaining the whole world, Nebuchadnezzar lost it all, only to be reminded that "only God is great!" Ask King Louis XIV.

Conclusions

1. To whom or to what shall we compare so great a Lord? He has no limits, no match, no rival, and no comparisons can even approach his likeness or being.
2. With so great a Lord, then, why do we in the Western world languish in such a theological, intellectual, moral, and ethical vacuum? Will not the Western powers fall just as decisively as the Eastern European powers fell—and for the same reasons?
3. Have we not walked in pride, and will God not humble us too if we do not renounce our sin and do what is right?
4. May our Lord help us to take the advice of the Spirit-empowered witness of Daniel and change, concluding that "only God is Great!"

3

MAGNIFYING THE WORD
OF OUR GOD

NUMBERS 20:1–13

Introduction

First, we must focus on the theology behind this text. Few subjects appear more frequently in the Bible than that of the "word" or "speech" of God. Fundamental to all biblical religion is the conviction that God has spoken and revealed himself in his word. It is through that word that we are able to come to know who God is and what his will and desire are for the individuals and families of the earth.

The word was never just a sound or mere talk; in the Old Testament a word often took on a reality not usually connected with a word in our times. This can be seen in formulae of blessing and cursing. Thus, when Jacob cheated his brother Esau out of his birthright, there does not appear to be any way their father could reverse his words once they were uttered (Gen. 27). The spoken word had gone forth, and that was that!

If this is how human words were regarded, how much more powerful and effective was God's word! More than that, it was a

word that would endure: "The word of our God stands forever" (Isa.
40:8; cf. 59:21). God's word could be a word of judgment (Hos. 6:5)
or a word of healing (Ps. 107:20).

God's word is expressed in a variety of ways in Scripture. He often
spoke through direct address, through theophanies (i.e., appear-
ances of God), through visions or dreams, or through messengers
who brought his words of grace, blessing, instruction, reproof, or
warning, or his direction for acting and living.

Of particular interest is the Hebrew construct phrase, *devar
YHWH*, "the word of the LORD [=Yahweh]," along with its coun-
terpart, *devar 'elohim*, "the word of God." Here was a message about
or, more frequently, from Yahweh/God. The former formula occurs
242 times in the singular and 17 times in the plural form, "words of
the LORD." Whatever else is true of the God of Israel, he certainly is a
God who speaks. The expression "thus says the LORD" is a hallmark
of the prophetic speeches. The prophets' messages are peppered with
this rubric. Moreover, the expression, "The word of the LORD came
to me," or some variation thereof, appears in the superscription of
eight of the sixteen prophetical books (Hos. 1:1; Joel 1:1; Jonah 1:1;
Mic. 1:1; Zeph. 1:1; Hag. 1:1; Zech. 1:1; and Mal. 1:1).

Israel was extremely privileged to have heard these words from the
LORD, for no other nation ever experienced the same (Exod. 20:22;
Deut. 4:33, 36). This speaking ability marked Yahweh as distinct
and superior to the false gods and idols of the nations, for they were
mute (Ps. 115:5; Isa. 41:26; Jer. 10:5).

While God revealed himself in the acts of the created world and in
history, it is his verbal declarations that teach us how to understand
this created order, the events of space and time, and who he is and
what he has done for us as mortals in need of redemption and guidance on how we should live and act. Such communication from God
was not meant to deflect us from coming to know the Almighty and
his plans for us, but was delivered to make him and his plan more
intelligible and understandable to mortals.

True, the Bible does not reflect on the psychology or the method-
ology that makes it possible for an infinite God to get his message
across to humans. Nevertheless, we are aware of God's condescension
in using human language—the language of Canaan and of the Greek

marketplace—to communicate. No one has ever claimed that this choice was one that would lead us to a comprehensive understanding of all that God is and could say to us; but it is an adequate means, as is demonstrated in the divine word's ability to get the message across generation after generation.

Accordingly, whether God's words are from the first conversation with Adam in the Garden of Eden, or are the promises found in the covenants formed with Abraham, Isaac, or Jacob, or are even the "ten words" of the Decalogue, they still come to us as fresh and as powerful as the day they were given. Those words reveal the character of God, as well as his plan and will for the nation Israel, through whom he has planned to gift and bless all the nations and Gentiles of the world (Gen. 12:3). It is from this word that we know God's promises, commands, judgments, and grace and the effects of disobedience. It is this word that men and women are to live by and to set the course of their lives in accordance with. God's people must not flaunt that word; rather, they are to meditate on it and make it their delight and hope for all the future (Ps. 119:11, 16, 97, 162; Jer. 15:16).

No wonder, then, that our Lord should be celebrated for his magnificent word. His words are invested with all of his authority, faithfulness, and sovereignty. Never are his words flawed or spotted with impurity, for God does not lie (Num. 23:19; Ps. 12:6; 18:30; Prov. 30:5). Since God's words come from him, they possess the same eternal character, the same purity, the same truthfulness, and the same integrity as he himself possesses (Ps. 119:89; Isa. 40:7–8). There are no exceptions to this characterization of the words of God, for even where some texts say that God "relented" or "repented" (Exod. 32:9–14; 1 Sam. 15:29; Isa. 38:1–6), they refer only to the fact that God was able to change in his reactions to women and men because they had changed or repented. Thus he was able to remain immutable in his character as he changed in his actions and responded to the change in mortals as they moved from disobedience to obedience.

To doubt or refuse to obey God's word is serious business indeed, for it is essentially to doubt or to reject God himself. Regardless of the means by which the word of God came—whether through a messenger like one of the prophets, a vision, a dream, or a direct speech from God—it was still rebellion and an outright rejection of his very person and authority to reject or refuse to obey what God had said through his prophet or oracle.

So powerful was this word from above that the prophet Jeremiah likened it to a "hammer that breaks the rock in pieces" (Jer. 23:29). All substitutes for this same word of God are as straw compared with real grain (Jer. 23:28). Therefore, there was a real divide between true prophets and the false prophets who spoke "visions from their own minds" (Jer. 23:16), or who ran with a "message [that God] did not speak to them" (Jer. 23:21). Other dead giveaways to their falseness were their lifestyles: "they commit adultery and live a lie" (Jer. 23:14), further "distort[ing] the words of the living God" (Jer. 23:36) by acts of plagiarism. They stole the real words of God from his true prophets and mixed them with their own words, deriving a message that was either false or distorted.

No wonder, then, when God told Moses to speak on the high authority of heaven to the rock to break out its water in Numbers 20, it was a most serious offense for Moses to slug the rock instead of merely speaking to it. The power and authority had to rest in the spoken word itself, as authorized by God, not in anything that Moses, Aaron, or anyone else could do. It is this background and theology of the word of God that will make this passage such a forceful representation of the magnificence and incomparable greatness of our God and his most effective and true word.

An Exposition of Numbers 20:1–13

When it gets hot, the first thing every person thinks of is a drink! My family was in such a situation some years ago as we were traveling south on Highway 128 north of Boston. As usual, that road was under construction, and we were moving up one car length at a time on a hot July day with the temperature at 95 degrees Fahrenheit. This was in the early 1960s and we had not yet gotten one of those air-conditioned cars, so all the windows were open, and we were trapped in three lanes of traffic. In antiphonal response to my hitting the brakes as I inched the car along, our two-year-old son called out from the backseat, "I want a 'gink'!" He could not say "drink" as yet. At first it was cute, but to hear that every ten seconds for an hour and a half is too much. After a while all of us wanted a "gink." My mouth felt like cotton. I could not wait until we could find a service station and get some kind of "gink."

Ancient Israel found itself in the same predicament: it was hot in the desert and the babies started to cry, "We want a 'gink.'" Add to that all the young children and older folks, along with the sheep and goats, as they joined in complaining about the fact that there was no water anywhere, and you have a recipe for disaster. It is precisely this situation that provides the setting for our narrative in Numbers 20:1–13.

It was the first month of the fortieth year of wandering in the wilderness. The whole preceding generation of rebels had died off (Num. 14:32–35), and it was now time for a whole new advance for the promises of God as the Israelites prepared to enter the promised land. But there still were some sorrows to traverse even in this fortieth year. The year had begun with Miriam's funeral (Num. 20:1), and before the middle of that fortieth year, the high priest Aaron also had passed on (Num. 20:22, 29). This does not sound like an auspicious beginning for a new advance into the promised land. To lose your key leaders just when you are about to take on the new challenges of conquering the land, settling it, and getting ready for all that needed to be done was not what most would have liked or planned. But Israel's help (and ours) has never depended solely on human hands, sagacity, or power to get things done; it rests (as always) with the living LORD.

A passage that starts with two funerals really sounds "dead"! And this message could likewise be moribund, except for the fact that it shines with a mighty demonstration of the power that resides in the magnificent word of God. Thus, while the experiences of mortals are cyclical, God's plan and work in history are not. True, Israel had been at this point before. Just after their journey out of Egypt had begun, they ran out of water at Massah (Exod. 17:1–7). One would think they would have remembered back forty years and said, "We will not make the same mistake our forefathers made when they too were out of water." But that did not happen. Instead, they complained as mightily as they could in rebellion against Moses and Aaron and against God.

This is why 1 Corinthians 10:1–15 takes three of the stories from this very same context in Numbers 16, 21, and 25 to teach us that "[the Israelites] all ate the same spiritual food and drank the same spiritual drink; for they drank from the spiritual rock that accompanied them, and that rock was Christ. Nevertheless, God was not pleased with most of them; their bodies were scattered over the desert" (1 Cor. 10:3–5). The apostle Paul drew warnings from these texts, since "these things occurred as examples, to keep us from setting our hearts on evil things as they did" (1 Cor. 10:6). Here were the lessons Paul drew from these texts:

"Do not be idolaters" (1 Cor. 10:7, 14)

"[Do] not commit sexual immorality" (1 Cor. 10:8; cf. Num. 25)

"[Do] not test the Lord" (1 Cor. 10:9; cf. Num. 21)

"Do not grumble (murmur)" (1 Cor. 10:10; cf. Num. 16)

Therefore, we turn to this passage with anticipation of a message that will help us to hold high the mighty word of God in all its magnificence.

The focal point, or big idea, of this passage is found in verses 8 and 10: "Speak to that rock before their eyes and it will pour out its water," and "Moses said to them, 'Listen you rebels, must *we* bring you water out of this rock?'" (emphasis mine). Accordingly, the title for our lesson or sermon will be "Magnifying the Word of Our God."

How do we magnify the word of our God in this text? Note that we will use the interrogative "how?" and the homiletical key word "ways." As a narrative text, the unit breaks down into four key scenes, giving us four ways that we can magnify the word of our God:

I. By Hearing His Word (Num. 20:2)

II. By Seeing His Word (Num. 20:3–5)

III. By Applying His Word (Num. 20:6–11)

IV. By Respecting His Word (Num. 20:12–13)

I. By Hearing His Word (Num. 20:2)

The power of God's word can be seen in the way it meets one of life's most basic needs: water (Num. 20:2)! But what Israel had learned from the past is about the same as what many of us learn from the past: nothing! We see in Exodus 17 that they had run out of water once before. Now here they were again. You can almost hear the doomsday predictors raining down on their brethren all sorts of cloudy assertions and once again blaming their leaders for all that was happening to them and calling for them to resign. After all, when your leader reaches 120 years of age, he ought to retire. So it was all Moses's fault; that is where the problem rested. It never occurred to any of them that they might be the problem instead.

The rowdy loudmouths griped and complained and refused to stop short of calling for an uprising against Moses and Aaron. This is when it is tough being a leader. One can understand Moses and Aaron's perspective: who needs all of this back talk and rebellion from a people you are trying to guide and deliver safely to their destination? The desert situation was serious enough without also having to face detractors. But God was once again testing Israel, just as we are often tested, to find out what was in their hearts. Had not the Lord led them all these forty years in the desert, humbling them and testing them "in order to know what was in [their] heart" (Deut. 8:2)? He had fed them with manna "to teach [them] that man does not live on bread alone but on every word that comes from the mouth of the LORD" (Deut. 8:3). Could it have been for any different reason here in the Desert of Zin near Kadesh that all of this was happening to them? What was their estimate of the word of God?

All too frequently we think that life consists of food and water, but that is to miss the mark by a good stretch. Mortals do not live by their intelligence, their reputation, their grandchildren's success, or by the fame anyone has achieved. No, real living begins and continues only when we are nourished daily by the words that come from the lips of our incomparably great God. Everything, including food and water, must take second place in the list of priorities. So, talk about human needs! We need God's word more than we need anything else, yet in most quarters that continues to be a scarce item. There is a huge famine of the word of God in our midst, even to this very day (Amos 8:11), because there is little or no practice of home Bible study and devotional reading of Scripture or of any consistent, solid, expositional preaching from many of the pulpits in our cities and towns. God's people are starving and dying on the vine because they are being given everything but the powerful word of God. We must have preaching and teaching that takes us chapter after chapter, paragraph after paragraph, and book after book through the sixty-six books of the Bible if this famine is to find any relief soon.

II. By Seeing His Word (Num. 20:3–5)

To make matters worse, Israel soon forgot all of God's previous deeds and interventions on their behalf. The attack on Moses's leadership continued as the Israelites said in essence, "The ol' gray Moses ain't what he used to be." They began to call down imprecations on their own heads, saying, "[We wish] we had died when our brothers fell dead before the LORD!" (v. 3). Did they really want to be swallowed up by the earth just as all of Korah's men had been consumed when the earth split open because of their opposition to Moses and the things of God (Num. 16:32–33)?

The prophet Amos would later issue a strong warning to those who in an insincere way said in effect, "We wish the day of the LORD were here" (Amos 5:18). "You don't even know what you are talking about," warned Amos. In effect he retorted, "Wait until you see what the day of the LORD is like for all who are unprepared for it because of being disobedient to the LORD." And so it should be said for all such braggadocios. The Israelites grumbled and fought with Moses about what they knew was not Moses's doing but God's actions in the past and present. The greatest favor ever done for any people, their deliverance from Egypt and preservation in the wilderness and the desert, was now drawing sneers and cynical remarks from those who had benefited from these divine actions.

The people mocked as they attributed their present state to Moses, for they pointedly said that he was the one who had brought them out of Egypt, along with their cattle—as they now let their cattle "horn in" on the argument and added them to the list as part of

Moses's now foiled deliverance. They brazenly suggested (in effect), "Skip the milk and the honey you promised us in this place we are supposed to be going to. We don't see any grain, figs, grapevines, or pomegranates. And worse still, mister, where's the water?"

It is enough to make a leader want to resign right then and there. You can almost hear Moses saying to himself (if this were a modern situation), "Why should I put up with all of this? I am not being paid any kind of big salary. I get no retirement benefits, no medical or dental benefits, so why am I doing all of this? I don't need it one bit!" The text does not say this, of course, but who would blame him if he did at least think something like this? He was unappreciated to the nth degree.

III. By Applying His Word (Num. 20:6–11)

Moses and Aaron's immediate reaction to this public rejection by those willing to speak out was to retreat to the tent of meeting and fall on their faces before God (v. 6). As a result of their action, "The glory of the LORD appeared to them" (v. 6b), and new instructions from God were given to Moses.

Faced with a potential mass revolt and widespread disobedience, Moses was to take his staff/rod and the two leaders were to assemble all Israel together in front of the rock there in that camp. So far, all was going well. But then God ordered Moses to "Speak to that rock" (v. 8), which was extraordinary enough. However, he was to speak to the rock "before [Israel's] eyes" (v. 8).

Now that could have been the end of everything. Here the people were opposing Moses and Aaron, feeling perhaps that both of them were "over the hill" and should have retired long ago. But now they would see Moses publicly talking to a rock, which would surely signal that the ol' boy had lost it for sure. God's promise was that water would come forth from the rock as a result of the verbal command of Moses given in the strong name of God. There would be water, Moses was assured, enough for the community and for their livestock.

We may wonder, Why this method? Why not send out teams to search for water holes or for springs? What could speaking do at a time like this? Actions, not words, were needed now!

However, therein lies the greatness and the majesty of our Lord. The people, as is so often true of us today, had doubted the power of the *word of God* and wanted to see some visible actions that would end their discomfort. The word of God, they judged, is all right for spiritual exercises and for days of worship, but not for the rough-and-tumble realities of the real world!

By this time, Moses had had just about enough. Even though it is always too soon to quit, he failed God at a critical moment. Surely the Lord knew how badly the children, adults, and even the cattle and herds needed water. Could God not hear the cries of the babies and the young children? "Water, Mother, water!" Even the sheep and goats seemed to mock God's leader as they bleated and fussed for water.

With all the congregation gathered in front of this rock, Moses decided to let them have a piece of his mind. He had had it with them. So he blurted out, "Listen, you rebels, must *we* bring you water out of this rock?" (v. 10).

Who said anything about Moses and Aaron bringing water out of the rock? God had worked so hard to set up this lesson so that this generation also might know that men and women do not live by water or food alone but by every word that comes out of the mouth of God; was Moses now about to spoil the plan? Wasn't the lesson more important even than water? The only connection between the extremity of their present need and the water provided was to be God's word. Speak the word! That is where they were critically deficient—as we are so often deficient as well. We truly are concerned about real needs and crises, but we want to meet them without involving the word of God. Yet that is precisely what is needed—no more, no less: his word!

In his anger, Moses raised his arm and let that rock have it; he socked it twice with his staff. Some say that in doing so he broke the typology that pointed to Christ, for our Lord, who elsewhere is given the metaphor of the "Rock," was only smitten on the cross "once for all." However, that cannot be what was wrong here. Later the psalmist had occasion to reflect on this same incident in Psalm 106:32–33. There he noted, "By the waters of Meribah they angered the LORD, and trouble came to Moses because of them; for they rebelled against the Spirit of God, and *rash words* came from Moses' lips" (italics mine). So, Moses did not break the type; rather, his fault was that he distrusted the power of the word of God. True, he was provoked, and the psalmist confirms that point. Nevertheless, he stole glory from God with just a little personal pronoun, "we." "Must *we* bring you water out of this rock?" Through the prophet Isaiah the Lord would later warn, "I am the LORD; that is my name! I will not give my glory to another" (Isa. 42:8). God's person and his word had to be set forth in front of a watching Israel as being altogether different and separate from the names, power, and speeches of others. We should never trivialize or make common what God has set apart as holy and separate, which in this place was his word.

The amazing result was that God still graciously gave the people water. I would have expected, after Moses and Aaron's major disobedience, that a voice would have come from heaven saying, "You are all rebels, including the leaders. No one listens to me or to my word. You still expect water? What do you think this is? I hope you all get good and thirsty, for none of you deserve any mercy, much less water!" But that speech did not take place. God graciously sent forth water so abundantly that it must have washed away the whole center of the line of angry demonstrators.

God is generous with his mercy and grace; yes, even in the Old Testament. Water came forth copiously. I was asked one time how much water the Israelites needed. I said I did not know, so the questioner pressed harder. How many people were there? I estimated over two million. How much water do they each need for drinking, washing, and cooking? I guessed about a gallon and a half minimum per day per person. How many sheep and goats were there? continued my interrogator. I said I did not know that either, but I would guess at least one for every other person, about one million. How much water do they consume in a day, I was quickly asked. I judged about two gallons each. My interrogator worked for the local water department, so he calculated the flow per second from the rock and concluded that water had to come out of that rock at something like 1,600 gallons per second! Now that really beat the Sunday school paper illustration I got when I was a kid, which pictured a little trickle that would have been consumed by the first

six people who took a drink! However much water it was, it had to
set a bunch of the protestors swimming with the enormous outflow
from that rock.

But how much more impressive would it have been had Moses
stuck to the word of God, letting a distrusting people see its effects
in all its power? Surely, we too suffer from a "trickle-down theology"
of the word. We too often expect too little when God wants to send
out a gigantic waterspout that will stagger the imagination of all
who behold it!

IV. By Respecting His Word (Num. 20:12–13)

Finally, God's word is true in all its sanctions and judgments.
God does not act like we mortals do, for he still quenches the thirst
of men and women and feeds us even when we do not deserve one
whit of his mercy and grace.

Even so, God's sentence against Moses and Aaron was immediate.
They had failed to "believe" and to "trust in [God] enough to honor
[him] as holy in the sight of the Israelites" (v. 12). While the crowd
was guilty of stirring Moses up, nevertheless, there is a double indemnity clause (James 3:1) for all leaders. They must be very careful
what they do for it has an effect not only on their own person, but
also much more seriously on those they lead. Moses had rebelled
directly against God's commandment (Num. 27:14). Did he doubt
that God's plan would really work? Did he think that the people were
so rebellious that it could not work?

Whatever his thinking, it all came down to a lack of belief in
God's word. Thus, the two leaders would now be denied the privilege
of leading this nation into the land of promise. Even though God
showed himself as holy on that day (v. 13), there were consequences
for the two leaders. Yes, there is *forgiveness* for all sin, but there are
still *consequences* from some of our deeds that cannot be reversed.
I may be forgiven of mugging someone, but if I permanently dam-
aged my victim's brain in so doing, the effect remains. That is why
the book of James speaks of a double indemnity clause for leaders.
Leaders are responsible both for themselves and for those they teach
or lead.

The warning is clear: leaders, pastors, teachers, and lay workers for the Lord must wrestle with their doubts on their knees privately in their homes and study rooms, but not in public. It is not proper to give vent publicly to our anger and our keen disappointment when people do not appreciate what we do for them. Note also that even great individuals tend to fall right in the area of their greatest strength. Here, one whom God called the humblest of mortals (Num 12:3) got caught in the white heat of his anger toward those rebels who egged him on. This was an area of his strength, yet it was in that same area that he fell. Gone was the meek disposition; in its place was white hot anger!

Moses, who so frequently delivered Israel as a mediator, now pleaded for himself on at least three or four occasions for God to rescind his sanction against him and let him take Israel into the land. But God said in effect, "No, it is enough; say no more" (Num. 27:12–14; Deut. 1:37; 3:22–26; 4:21; 32:51).

Aaron too was sanctioned by God and was "gathered to his people" (Num. 20:24) as he and Moses ascended Mount Hor, near the border of Edom. There Moses removed from Aaron his garments and dressed Aaron's son, Eleazar, with the vestments of the office, continuing the line of the office of high priest. This demonstrated the transitory nature of the ceremonial law. Aaron's line of the priesthood would not endure forever, for Christ's priesthood would replace Aaron's line and would be patterned after another, the order of Melchizedek (Heb. 7:11–24).

Mercy came to the people, but what a cost it brought to them all as they were forced to go on without the leaders who had communicated God's word to them for the past forty years.

Conclusions

1. God's word stands firm and true whether we allow it to work or not. It is no excuse to protest that our desperations, our inconveniences, and our crises take precedence over the word of God. They do not, nor should they ever be thought to even come close to rivaling it.

2. Mortals can only really live if they live by the word of God. That is where living begins and how it is able to go on. So we must trust God's word, especially if we lead.

3. Even when leaders are provoked, they must still stay on message and on course. They are God's gifts to his people and are there for the good of God's people (Heb. 13:7, 17).

4. God can and does forgive, but he also must attach consequences to disobedience, especially for leaders. Psalm 99:8 warns that even though God is a forgiving and pardoning God, he still must punish Israel for their misdeeds.

5. No one was ever forgiven without someone paying—even in the everyday events where others ask us to forgive them. In effect they do not ask us to just gloss over the matter, but they want us to take on the onus of paying for what they did wrong, if we forgive them. That is what our heavenly Father does for us when he forgives us.

May we have a whole new regard for the word of this great God. His word alone can bring back life and real living to the hungry masses, and his word alone can break the logjams and the impediments that have blocked the free flow of the power of God to a watching and sin-sick world.

4

MAGNIFYING THE WONDERFUL NAME OF OUR GOD

JEREMIAH 32:1–44

Introduction

In order to prepare for the exposition of Jeremiah 32:1–44, I have chosen to set the scene by focusing on the magnificent "name" of God and especially on one of his names, "Wonderful." The in-depth look at both of these terms from the perspective of a word study and a biblical theological approach should deepen our appreciation for what is going on in this text and add immeasurably to the depth with which we can exalt the magnificence of the wonderful name of our Lord.

Names in the ancient world of the Semites were more than mere marks of identification or forms of addressing others.[1] More often than not, they were descriptions of character or reflected the conditions under which the name was given. Even more significant was the fact that often the naming act itself brought the things named into existence. That is because the things named would be seen to be so closely identified with the object described that failure to have a name was like ceasing to exist and being cut off from the land of the living. Therefore, the naming process was by no means casual, especially in the earlier parts of the Old Testament.

The act of naming was an act of dominion as well. Consider how in the creation story God named the heaven, earth, dry land, and the like and thereby showed his sovereignty over the created order. Nothing demonstrated the fact that he was the author and creator of the stuff of the universe more than the fact that he named it, which also showed he was owner and lord over it all. Parents have the right to name their own children because they are the parents of those children. True, the kids or neighbors down the street may call our children by other names, but those are not their real names; other people have no right to name our children or to exercise dominion over them. But God has that right, and he is sovereign over all. This Lord also gave the task of naming the animals to Adam, thereby giving Adam dominion over the animal world.

But *name* also refers to one's reputation. Did God not promise to make Abraham's name/reputation great (Gen. 12:2)? Did not our Lord repeat the same promise to David (2 Sam. 7:9)? Proverbs 22:1 notes that "a good name is more desirable than riches; to be esteemed is better than silver or gold." In this proverb, having "a good name" is parallel to being "esteemed," thereby showing how name, esteem, and reputation are closely linked ideas.

Closely related to this concept of reputation is that of "fame." In Genesis 6:4 the "men of renown," or literally "men of a name," were seeking fame or desiring to become "famous." No less involved in the same objective were those in Genesis 11:4, where the men who were building the tower of Babel were desirous of "mak[ing] a name for [themselves]." They too sought fame and a reputation.

A name also can refer to the attributes or character of the one named. Thus in Exodus 34:5–7 the Lord declares his name, which is followed immediately by a list of divine attributes: He is "Lord," "compassionate," "gracious," "slow to anger," "abounding in love and faithfulness/grace and truth," and more. Another case where the Lord's name (or names) signifies the very essence of his character is Isaiah 9:6b: "And he will be called Wonderful Counselor, Mighty God, Everlasting Father, Prince of Peace." It is the first of these four names that we wish to focus on in this passage, where our Lord is seen as "Wonderful."

Twice in Jeremiah 32 (in vv. 17 and 27) a form of the Hebrew verb *pale'* occurs with the meaning, "to be difficult, to be hard, to be extraordinary, to be wonderful, to be marvelous." This root points to what is judged to be extraordinary and wonderful when measured against what we normally expect or what we are accustomed to. Such events evoke astonishment and immediate praise from those who behold them, for they are simply so outstanding that they fall outside the class of the ordinary.

When used in a religious context, this word (or its passive participle form) is most frequently connected with God, especially his acts of salvation. The exodus event is one of those extraordinary works of God where this acclamation of "wonderful" is used (Exod. 3:20; Mic. 7:15). Add to that the crossing of the Red Sea (Ps. 78:12–14) and the crossing of the Jordan River (Josh. 3:5), and all these events start falling into a class that is surely outside the usual or ordinary. They all are "wonderful."

God is celebrated as "the One who alone does wonders" (Job 5:9; 9:10; Ps. 72:18; 86:10; 98:1; 105:5; 106:22; 136:4; Neh. 9:17). In fact, all of God's works can be classified as "wonderful" (his laws, Ps. 119:129; his work in the final day, Dan. 12:6; his governance and judgments in the world, Isa. 25:1; and his work in nature and creation, Job 9:10; 37:5).

Despite all the wonderful acts of God recorded in the Pentateuch, only two texts in those first five books celebrate our Lord and his acts as "wonders," or "wonderful" (Exod. 3:20; 34:10). However, the hymnic sections of the Old Testament, especially the Psalms, emphasize this subjective experience that God's acts produce in those who behold such "wonders," showing that they were indeed seen as clearly being out of the ordinary and evoking a sense of awe and mystery.

God's purpose in bringing these acts of wonder to the hearts and minds of his people is to call them to faith (Ps. 78:32) or even to reflection and thought (Job 37:14). These wonders must be "proclaimed" (1 Chron. 16:24; Ps. 9:1[2]; 26:7; 75:1[2]; 78:4; 96:3), "remembered" (1 Chron. 16:12; Ps. 105:5), "meditated on" (Ps. 105:2; 119:27; 145:5),

and "extolled" (Ps. 89:5[6]; 107:8; 139:14). They all lead to the exalta-
tion of the majesty and magnificence of our God.

With this word study moving across biblical times (diachronic-
ally), we are ready to look at this amazing chapter in the book of
Jeremiah.

An Exposition of Jeremiah 32:1-44

This chapter in Jeremiah belongs to the section of the book com-
monly referred to as the "Book of Consolation." Even though some
incorrectly limit the Book of Consolation to Jeremiah 30 and 31,
the same themes of promise and hope for restoration of Judah and
Israel extend through chapters 32 and 33; therefore I, along with the
majority of commentators, regard all of Jeremiah from chapter 30
through 33 as the Book of Consolation. The emphasis in Jeremiah
30 and 31, to be sure, is on the *future* of the nation, whereas chapters
32 and 33 emphasize a return to the *land* as a sign of the restoration
of Israel's fortunes.

Jeremiah 32 has as its specific time the events that occurred just
before the fall of Jerusalem in 587 BC, when the prophet was confined
to the "courtyard of the guard" (32:2). This had to be the darkest
moment in all of Israel's history, yet it was precisely against this
desperate backdrop that God had Jeremiah issue his assurance of
restoration to the land God had promised long ago to give to Abraham, Isaac, and Jacob.

The year was 588 BC, the tenth year of the Judean king Zedekiah.
Nebuchadnezzar, now in the eighteenth year of his reign, had placed
a siege on the city of Jerusalem, where the prophet Jeremiah had
been imprisoned in the palace area.

During this time the Lord's word came to Jeremiah, instruct-
ing him to purchase some of the family inheritance by redeeming
the land that apparently otherwise would be bought out from the
family because of debts or other problems. The purchase of this
land in his hometown of Anathoth would be a symbolic action of
Jeremiah, similar to other actions he had previously taken under
the direction of God, such as wearing and then hiding the linen

belt (Jer. 13:1–4), abstaining from marriage (16:1–13), visiting the potter's house (18:1–12), and smashing the pottery vessel (19:1–5). Thus a concrete visualization of the prophet's message through these symbolic actions became another means by which God tried to get his message across to his people.

The focal point of this passage comes in verses 17–18: "Nothing is too hard/too wonderful for you [Lord]. . . . O great and powerful God, whose name is the LORD Almighty." Accordingly, the subject of our teaching or preaching on this passage is "Magnifying the Wonderful Name of Our God."

The following structure of this narrative text exhibits its divisions with brief descriptions of the four settings or scenes:

32:1–15: The visit of cousin Hanamel; the offer to purchase land

32:16–25: Jeremiah's prayer after purchasing the land

32:26–35: God's word about his anger over Judah's sin

32:36–44: God's promise to restore Israel to her land in the future

The interrogative that helps to move from the particulars of these unique events to the generalized principles for all times and all cultures is the question "what?" The homiletical key word will be "aspects," for there are four aspects of the wonderful name of God that we should magnify and exalt in true worship and joy for the Lord who is disclosed here. Those four aspects are:

I. Our God Is Wonderful in His Word (Jer. 32:1–15)
II. Our God Is Wonderful in His Person (Jer. 32:16–25)
III. Our God Is Wonderful in His Wrath (Jer. 32:26–35)
IV. Our God Is Wonderful in His Promises (Jer. 32:36–44)

I. Our God Is Wonderful in His Word (Jer. 32:1–15)

The story that the prophet is about to tell here appears to be connected to events related in Jeremiah 37:11–21, where Jeremiah is arrested for what was perceived to be his desertion of the city of

Jerusalem. But apparently he was simply going about two miles north of Jerusalem to his hometown of Anathoth to see the property he had just purchased.

But that is getting ahead of our story. In chapter 32, Jeremiah is at pains to set for us the precise time when all the following events occurred. It was the tenth year of the Judean king Zedekiah's reign and the eighteenth year of the Babylonian king Nebuchadnezzar's reign. Jerusalem was already under siege, and Jeremiah was confined to quarters in the palace area.

The events of Jeremiah 32 begin with the Judean king accusing Jeremiah of treason for what he had been prophesying. Zedekiah makes a long accusation (vv. 3–5) and complains particularly about Jeremiah claiming that his words were from the Lord. How could *God* be the agent who would "hand this city over to the king of Babylon," when it was also said that *Nebuchadnezzar* was the one who would "capture it [the city]" (v. 3)? How could any real patriot of Judah say there was no use fighting Babylon and that any such resistance would "not succeed" (v. 5)? The question is left hanging in the air with no response from God or the prophet except the symbolic action that immediately follows.

God alerts the prophet that his cousin Hanamel will arrive at the "courtyard of the guard" at the royal palace with a request that Jeremiah purchase his uncle's field in Anathoth. Since Jeremiah is the closest relative, he can redeem the property (vv. 7–8). This is a most unexpected request for two reasons: (1) the country was under attack by the Babylonians, so, while prices were probably way under market value, what was the use of owning anything when the Babylonians would soon own it all; and (2) Jeremiah's relationship with the family was strained, to say the least, since they had judged him to be crazy (Jer. 11:18–23; 12:6). Had there been a reconciliation with the family in the meantime, or were they so desperate that they had to put their pride away and humbly beg Jeremiah to bail out the family inheritance?

Leviticus 25:25–28 provided for the right of a family member to redeem property that had to be sold for financial or other distressing reasons. Whether that was fully operative here or not we cannot say, but surely some aspects of it were. Although the family despised

Jeremiah, they had to appeal to him as their last resort. They had to eat humble pie and beg a man they deemed to be a lowly prophet to bail the family inheritance out of debt by paying off the most recent purchaser of the land, who was not a family member. In God's economy, the land had to remain in perpetuity in the family line, and it could not be sold or used as collateral.

"Just as the LORD had said" (v. 8), Hanamel came to Jeremiah with this very request. That is how Jeremiah "knew that this was the word of the LORD" (v. 8d). Jeremiah "weighed out for him seventeen shekels of silver" (v. 9), which is about seven ounces. Notice these were not coins, for coins were not invented until the Persian period late in the sixth century BC. At our current value of silver, somewhere near $13.00 an ounce, the field cost Jeremiah about $91.00. The prophet then "signed and sealed the deed" (v. 10) in the presence of witnesses. The "unsealed copy," or "open copy," replicated exactly what the sealed scroll said, but in case of a dispute, the sealed copy could be opened to verify the terms of the unsealed copy.

Jeremiah gave both copies to his secretary, Baruch, since the prophet was confined to the palace prison (vv. 12–13). We assume that Jeremiah must have been stopped as he attempted to leave Jerusalem during a brief interlude in the siege of the city to inspect his purchase, as Jeremiah 37:11–21 seems to indicate. However, the guards of the city assumed that Jeremiah was attempting to desert and to go over to the enemy that he seemed to favor in his preaching, so he was prevented from going to Anathoth and was imprisoned once again. Accordingly, Jeremiah gave Baruch both copies of the deed and instructed him to put them "in a clay jar so they will last a long time. For this is what the LORD Almighty, the God of Israel says: Houses, fields and vineyards will again be bought in this land" (vv. 14–15). The impending tragedy of the Babylonian conquest would not be the end of the story. The prophet was investing in the distant future, because God would return the people some day back to this same land. Thus the entire episode comes into theological focus as God delivers his word "again" in verse 15.

It is worth noting that sealed documents, such as the one Jeremiah has just completed, contained a *bulla* (a stamp seal) impression in soft clay that, once it hardened, sealed the document. Around 1986 a *bulla* was discovered that read "belonging to Berechiah, son of Neriah, the scribe."[2] Berechiah (which means "blessed of Yah[weh]") is the longer spelling of the shortened "Baruch," which means "blessed." Since the name of the father is the same ("Neriah") and the title of "scribe" is the same, this *bulla* could well be from Jeremiah's secretary, though there is nothing to connect it with the "deed of purchase" mentioned in this text.

This whole transaction must have impressed Jeremiah as being really out of character for him, for had he not, by now, preached for forty years about the fall of the nation? Why would anyone in his or her right mind buy real estate at a moment like this? It could likewise have struck Jeremiah as being more than foolish—unless he also believed the ancient promises of God! No wonder he will begin his prayer in the next section with a confession that also calls for faith: "Nothing is too hard/wonderful for you [Lord]" (v. 17). The fact that God's word is nothing short of "wonderful" is demonstrated by the events in this scene. Had not the prophet been told in advance about the proposal of his cousin, and were not the details exactly as God had revealed them? How much more wonderful can God's word get than that?

II. Our God Is Wonderful in His Person (Jer. 32:16–25)

After the field purchase transaction was completed, Jeremiah broke out into prayer to God. Answering prayer is still one of the chief ways in which God shows how mighty he really is. Jeremiah knew this very well, for in Jeremiah 33:3 he heard God say, "Call to me and I will answer you and tell you great and unsearchable things you do not know." Thus, for Jeremiah, as well as for us, there is no help for troubled hearts like prayer.

This is one of only two times Jeremiah prays in this the longest book in the Old Testament. Here Jeremiah prays especially for personal guidance; in Jeremiah 42:4 he asks for guidance for others as to whether they should move down to Egypt or not. But that is the totality of his prayers in this book, where God told him it was no use praying for this people, for they had long ago exhausted his mercy and grace (Jer. 7:16; 11:14; 14:11).

Jeremiah begins his prayer with "Ah, Sovereign LORD." The words seem to express dismay and are found in three other passages: one at his call (Jer. 1:6), and the others when the optimistic prophets claimed to have the truth but their message was different from what Jeremiah had been told (4:10; 14:13).

However, despite any and all feelings to the contrary, was not the Lord to whom Jeremiah now appealed the same one who stretched out the heavens and earth by his mighty arm? So why would anyone doubt that this God is the God of all wonders? What in heaven or on earth could prove to be too "wonderful" or "too hard and difficult" for him?

God's very name is "Wonderful" (Hebrew *pele'*, or the verb *pale'*). Was he not the same one who appeared as an angel and spoke to Samson's parents, asking why they requested his name seeing that it is "Wonderful" (Judg. 13:18)? And did not the Lord raise this same question for Abraham's wife Sarah? Despite the fact that she was ninety years of age, she would have a son, so God's question to doubting Sarah was, "Is anything too hard/wonderful for the Lord?" (Gen. 18:13–14). Wasn't that the name also given to Jesus in Isaiah 9:6? His name would be "Wonderful Counselor." And for those who doubted a restoration of Israel back to her land in the end days, God, through the prophet Zechariah, had to ask: " 'It may seem marvelous/wonderful/difficult to the remnant of this people at that time, but will it seem marvelous/wonderful/difficult to me?' declares the LORD Almighty" (Zech. 8:6).

The prayer of the prophet continues in Jeremiah 32:18 as he acknowledges that God is wonderful in his love and grace. In fact, as Jeremiah goes along in this prayer, it is a veritable outline of theology. He begins with God's power and grace in creation (v. 17) and adds God's boundless grace in the forgiveness of sin (v. 18). Then he magnifies the wisdom and works of God in carrying out his purposes and plans (vv. 19–23). Among those deeds God has singled out, Jeremiah notes how God is omniscient and can see and reward every mortal according to how he or she has acted. He also specifies that the great work of God is the exodus from Egypt and the conquest of the land of Canaan.

The person of our Lord is magnificent beyond description. All his works and all his attributes show how wonderful he is. There is nothing that he cannot do within the perfection of his person, plan, and characteristics. Our God is an awesome God.

III. Our God Is Wonderful in His Wrath (Jer. 32:26–35)

In this section God will finally answer Jeremiah's prayer and the "why?" of King Zedekiah (vv. 3–5), with the introductory word "therefore" (v. 28). Essentially the answer is that Israel and Judah needed to go through the fires of judgment before they could move into a future filled with the hope of the ancient promises.

God repeats Jeremiah's affirmation in verse 17, only here the Lord puts it in the form of a question: "Is anything too hard/marvelous/difficult for me?" (v. 27). The implied and expected answer, of course, is "No," but God cannot simply intervene at this point and call a halt to the threatened and impending disaster outside the city gates. The explanation of why Judah may not expect the immediate intervention of God is that they have not yet dealt with their unconfessed and cherished sins (vv. 28–29). This nation has been in the habit of provoking God ever since her youth (v. 30). They have repeatedly turned their backs on the Lord and substituted Baal and Molech for the Living God (vv. 33–35). This is what has excited the anger of God. If he did not deal with sin, the righteous would begin to think evil and wrong were enthroned as norms and that good and righteousness were now out of vogue. That is why the city (v. 28) must be handed over to the Babylonians. So Judah should not expect God to show his miracle-working, marvelous deeds or his love of doing what to others seems too hard and too difficult. Evil has had a free ride for too long, and it must be halted in its tracks as of now.

Surely our God is awesome in his wrath and in his judgment of evil and wickedness. A God of love must be one who, as C. S. Lewis said in describing true love, condones the least of our faults and sins, yet who also forgives us more than all of our critiques put together when we come to him asking for forgiveness. The Judahites must stop thinking that disaster will never come on Jerusalem just because it is the city where God dwells. They must stop saying that it could never happen here, because of God's promises. God, of course, would still fulfill his promises, but he would not necessarily have to do so with that generation.

IV. Our God Is Wonderful in His Promises (Jer. 32:36–44)

Despite the litany of judgments that God had just leveled against Judah, he now traces a most remarkable future with another "therefore" (rendered "but" in the NIV) in the Hebrew text of verse 36. Six wonderful promises are announced with mind-boggling implications for the distant future of Israel.

First of all, God promises that he will "surely gather them from all the lands where I banish them" (v. 37a). It is interesting to note that the Lord did not limit the land of banishing simply to Babylon. Instead, he mentioned all the lands where his people had gone. Restoration was still in the program and plan of God for Israel.

Second, not only would the people be returned to their own land, but God also would "let them live in safety" (v. 37b) in their land. Whatever restorations Israel has seen in history thus far have lacked one essential ingredient: safety. To this day, Israel is a nation obsessed with the great quest for safety.

A third promise (v. 38) essentially repeats the formula of the promise-plan of God that began way back in Genesis 17:7, where God pledged to be the people's God. The second part of this tripartite formula (the full rendering of which is: "I will be your God, you shall be my people, and I will dwell in the midst of you") was added in Exodus 6:7, where the Lord also promised to adopt them as his own people.

Add to these three promises another: "I will give them singleness of heart and action, so that they will always fear me for their own good and the good of their children after them" (v. 39). But when in the history of Israel, past or present, was Israel ever unified in its desire to fear God with no deviations one way or the other? This must refer to an eschatological day when life has been drastically changed, a day in which the hearts of the people have been revolutionized and revived.

Another blessing that came as a wonderful promise was that God would "make an everlasting covenant with them" (v. 40a).

This seems to reiterate what Jeremiah had called in his previous chapter the "new covenant" (Jer. 31:31–34). This new covenant was the continuation of the Abrahamic-Davidic covenant, but now it is called "everlasting," for its promises were to go on into eternity. Since it is eternal, God affirmed that he would "never stop doing good to them" and he would "inspire them to fear me, so that they will never turn away from me" (v. 40b). This is amazing in every detail, to say the least. God's plan for Israel, as it is for all the people of God worldwide, is one that has never gone off course or changed. It has always been and always will be his "everlasting covenant."

In the sixth and final wonderful promise, God declares that he "will rejoice in doing them good and will assuredly plant them in this land" (v. 41). Then he adds, most uniquely—for it is found nowhere else in the Bible—that he would plant them in their own land "with all my heart and soul" (v. 41b). We are accustomed to hearing mortals say, "I promise you with all my heart and soul," but never, until this point in the Bible, has God ever said anything like this. This must be an extremely important promise that our Lord wanted to underline in a major way. It is as if the Lord signed this promise about the restoration with his own name and with all the integrity of his being.

This wonderful set of promises ends with the contrast between the enormity of the coming calamity set over against the awesomeness of the promised prosperity of the people once they had gotten past this judgment. Now it makes sense why God had told Jeremiah to purchase that homestead field, for the day was coming when more deeds for fields, lands, and houses would again be signed and sealed (v. 44). God would "restore their fortunes" once more (44d).

Isn't it plain why the very name and character of God are seen so beautifully and so magnificently in his name "Wonderful"? Disaster had to come, given the intransigence of the people and the hardness of their hearts, but in no way will these calamities have the last word; God himself will have that last word in six magnificent and wonderful promises that more than spell out the truth that "His Name is Wonderful!"

Conclusions

1. In all of our stressful and busy lives, what would we offer as an illustration that here was something that was too hard, too difficult, too marvelous, for the Lord to handle and to give a solution for its resolution?
2. The invitation to pray is still open; we must call on the Lord. He has promised to answer us (Jer. 33:3) and show us great and mighty things we have not yet known or even thought possible.
3. Let us say all over again: his name, his works, his trademark is "wonderful." God can do anything that is not logically inconsistent with his being or that does not contradict the perfection of all of his other attributes. So let us not limit to our own abilities and initiatives the working of God in our lives, homes, marriages, churches, institutions, countries, and the gospel mandate. His abilities and initiatives supersede all of ours combined and more, for his name is "Wonderful."

5

Magnifying the Pardoning Grace of Our God

Micah 7:11–20

Introduction

"How were persons saved and pardoned for their sins in the Old Testament?" This is a question whose answer is not too readily available these days—not because the Old Testament did not treat this subject, but rather because few have taught the wonderful words that rang with hope and assurance in the earlier testament.

Even those who have some acquaintance with the message of the Old Testament still see problems that appear to be irreconcilable. For example, what are we to do with the pledge to "forgive" sin in the Old Testament and the equally strong affirmation that God will not let the guilty go unpunished? Can these two ideas be reconciled even before we reach the revelation of the New Testament? These and other questions must be faced before we can appreciate the wonderful pardoning grace of our God in Micah 7:11–20.

The word translated in the Old Testament as "pardon" or "forgive" comes from the Hebrew word *nasa'*, a root with a wide range of meanings, depending on the context, but whose basic idea is "to lift," "to carry," or "to bear." The literal sense can be seen in Genesis 7:17, where the floodwaters "lifted" up the ark of Noah.

However, when connected to contexts of sin, this word took on a sense of "lifting up," "bearing," or "pardoning" the penalty or price for one's sin. Here is where the idea of "pardon" and "forgiveness" entered the meaning set for this verb and noun. It was really in the Day of Atonement ceremonies that we begin to see the full range of this figurative sense, such as where the scapegoat "carri[ed] (Hebrew *nasa*) on itself all [Israel's] sins" (Lev. 16:22). Just as surely did our Lord, as the Servant of the Lord, "take on" or "carry" our infirmities (Isa. 53:4). Since John the Baptist was probably thinking in his Hebrew tongue as he spoke Aramaic (or was he using Greek at the time?), he proudly announced, "Look, the Lamb of God, who *takes away* the sin of the world" (John 1:29).

But all of this is getting ahead of our story. Let us begin at the Day of Atonement to get a better picture of what was happening in the Old Testament when sins were forgiven. The Day of Atonement has been called "the holiest Jewish holiday." Some might say the Passover rivaled it, yet none of the other Jewish festivals compared to the holiness of the ritual that pervaded the entire Day of Atonement.

But what does it mean "to atone?" The Hebrew verb form is *kipper*, rendered "to make atonement" (the noun form is *kippur*, from which we get the name *Yom Kippur*, "Day of Atonement"). So what does the word *atonement* mean? And what did it entail and signify when the people of the Old Testament "made an atonement"?

The word *atonement* seems to be an artificial English word created by dividing the word into its constituent parts: "at-one-ment" (using the abstract ending "ment"). Thus it means "the state of" seeing God and man "at one," or reconciled and in harmony with one another.

What then does "to make atonement" mean? Among the views suggested are: (1) "to wipe clean," "to purify," or "to cleanse"; (2) "to cover" or "to conceal"; and (3) "to ransom or deliver by means of a substitute."

The first meaning depends on a term judged to be an equivalent term in Akkadian, meaning "to wipe off," "to clean objects."[1] One author who espoused this view believed that the mercy seat, or the lid on the ark of the covenant in the temple, was a polluted object that needed to be wiped clean. But how could such an object dwell in the presence of God in the holy of holies? The ritual of this ceremony did not feature cleansing or wiping something clean. This cannot be the correct meaning when the subject is the sin of mortals.

A more popular view is that the sins of the Old Testament saints who believed in the Messiah were "covered"[2] or at least "concealed" (as is the case in its Arabic equivalent) until the time of Jesus's death on the cross, which paid sin's penalty. However, in only one context in the Old Testament does this verb have this meaning. It is used for caulking the ark with pitch so as to waterproof it in Genesis 6:14. Nowhere else does this word carry such a sense. And the Old Testament equally stresses the fact that our sins are removed (Ps. 103:12, "as far as the east is from the west, so far has he removed our transgressions from us"). Also, if "to cover" were the correct meaning, it makes it seem as if atonement in the Old Testament was just a cover-up job rather than a release and setting free from the weight and burden of sin.

A much better rendering and explanation is that *kipper* means "to pay a ransom," or "to deliver by a substitute."[3] These verbs are derived from the noun, in this case, *kofer*, meaning "ransom." Often the things (in the noun situation) ransomed were done so by offering a substitute. Therein lies the great teaching of what it means "to make an atonement." A substitute is offered to pay for the forgiveness of the person freed.

Note that nowhere in the Old Testament does it say that the blood of sheep, goats, or bulls atoned for anyone's sin. Instead, forgiveness was based on the declared word of God and rested on the fact that the Son of God would later come to offer his life as a substitute in payment for what each of the forgiven should have, but could not have, paid.[4]

So much for what the name of this important festival means. But how shall we understand the symbolism and the events that go on in this ritual on the Day of Atonement?

First of all, there was the preparation according to Leviticus 16:1–4. Aaron, the high priest at the time, also was a sinner and needed his sins pardoned before he could enter into ministry for anyone else. Therefore, he needed first to receive God's forgiveness before he could lead this ceremony. He had to select a young bull and a ram as a burnt offering to be offered on his own behalf. After he had bathed himself, he put on special sacred garments and entered the holy of holies in the tabernacle (later it will be the temple), and then entered the Holiest Place in the tabernacle one time every year "to make atonement" for himself and his household. Unlike the coming Messiah, he was not spotless and free of all sin, hence the need for his own personal preparation.

The priestly procedure that the high priest was to follow is found in Leviticus 16:11–14. The bull that the high priest offered for his own sin had to be slaughtered as his personal substitute (16:11). He was to approach the "atonement cover" over the ark of the covenant, between the cherubim, with a "censer full of burning coals . . . and two handfuls of finely ground fragrant incense," so the "smoke of the incense will conceal the atonement cover above the Testimony" (16:12–13). Then Aaron was to place "some of the bull's blood" on that cover and sprinkle some of it seven times before the place of atonement (16:14).

After the high priest had received forgiveness for his own sins, he emerged from the holy of holies to choose two male goats as a sin offering for the whole congregation and a ram for a burnt offering (Lev. 16:5). The lot was cast to determine which goat was to represent which part of the one sin offering: one goat to act as the substitute for all Israel's sins, that is, for all who truly repented and showed godly sorrow for their sins; and the other, a "scapegoat," or more accurately, the "goat-of-sending-away" (Hebrew *azazel*), to represent the removal of those sins far away from their lives or memory (16:8). This was not an offering to a demon, named Azazel, or to the devil, or anything like that. This was to show that the one sin offering had two parts.

After Aaron had confessed all the sin of all Israel over the head of the first goat—but only for those who had "humbled themselves" or "afflicted their souls" (Lev. 16:29, 31; 23:27, 29, 32, translated "deny [them]selves" in the NIV, or as we would say, who were truly sorry for their sins)—he would then slaughter the goat, which stood now as the people's stand-in substitute. The laying of hands on the head of the animal surely symbolized the transference of guilt from the offenders to the goat. This is what is meant by a vicarious atonement. It is the principle of an innocent substitute given on behalf of the guilty party.

To continue the drama of this Day of Atonement, once again the high priest entered the tabernacle's holy of holies, this time with the blood of the slaughtered goat. He was to do the same thing with its blood that he had done with the bull's blood when he sought forgiveness for his own sin. Thus he made atonement for the people, but in picture form that graphically illustrated what Christ would later do for all who repented of their sin when he became our substitute and paid the penalty that was due to each one of us.

Finally, Aaron would emerge from the tabernacle and once again confess all the sin of all Israel, of all who were truly sorry for their sin, over the head of the second goat. The substitutionary part was now finished and this second part represented the fact that Israel's sins would be removed from them as far as the east is from the west (Ps. 103:12). That second goat was given to a man who led it into the wilderness as far as he could so that it got lost forever, never to return (Lev. 16:21–22). That is how God regards sins he has forgiven, the payment for which he has assumed responsibility. Not only were the sins of Israel forgiven on the basis of a substitute, but they were forgotten and remembered against Israel no more.

It is also important to grasp the meaning of "blood" in these Scriptures. Still more importantly, we must grasp what we mean when we talk about the blood of Christ. The phrase "blood of Christ," for example, is used in the New Testament three times more often than the "cross of Christ" and five times more frequently than the term the "death of Christ."[5] The prevalent, but incorrect, interpretation is that the blood of Christ stands for the setting free of his life for new purposes. However, the blood of the Savior refers to Christ's death as a sacrifice and a payment for our sin. The fundamental idea is not the bestowing of life or the releasing of life (as in a transfusion); it is the destruction of the seat of life, and hence it stands for death.[6] In three places the Old Testament teaches that the "life is in the blood" (Gen. 9:4; Lev. 17:11; Deut. 12:23), but these texts do not teach that the blood is life in isolation; instead, they teach that the blood is the life of all flesh. If the blood is separated from the flesh, whether in man or beast, the physical life of the flesh comes to an end. Blood, therefore, stands not for the release of life, as some have contended, but for the bringing to an end of life in the flesh.

All of this is a requisite background for appreciating Micah 7:11–20. So it is time to examine another text that magnifies the Lord God as the one who freely gives his incomparably great pardoning grace to all who believe.

An Exposition of Micah 7:11–20

Without a doubt, the focal point, or big idea, is found in verse 18 of this chapter, which says, "Who is a God like you, who pardons sin and forgives the transgression of the remnant of his inheritance?" Who, indeed, can even begin to come close to what our God is and does, for he exceeds every comparison, known and unknown. And he exceeds especially in the area of pardoning and forgiving our sins in this context. What a magnificent Lord!

Therefore, we ask, what (our interrogative) are the three *evidences* (our homiletical key word) of the incomparability of God's pardoning power in this text? They can be seen as follows:

I. In His Answer to Our Tormentors (Mic. 7:11–13)
   A. When New Walls Are Built
   B. When New Boundaries Are Set
   C. When People's Deeds Demand a Divine Response
II. In His Marvelous Deeds for Us (Mic. 7:14–17)
   A. Of Shepherding Us
   B. Of Working Miracles
   C. Of Conquering Nations
III. In His Forgiveness of Our Sins (Mic. 7:18–20)
   A. Based on Who He Is
   B. Based on What He Has Done

I. In His Answer to Our Tormentors (Mic. 7:11–13)

A. *When New Walls Are Built.* Still reverberating in the ears of Micah's listeners were the jeers and mocking of unbelievers who castigated Micah and the believers of his day with this assault: "Where is the LORD your God?" (Mic. 7:10). But God's response was to give a whole new set of evidences that spoke of another "day" (7:11[2x], 12). Thus, the full vindication of God would come in eschatological times in the distant future.

Meanwhile, God would show himself just as powerful as he really is and will be in his saving acts in the here and now.

In the overarching story of the Bible, God's people had felt the shame and frustration when the walls of Jerusalem were breached. To them, it felt as if the whole program of God and his salvation to all men had been stalled or forfeited, as in the story of Nehemiah (1:3) in 445 BC, when he too found the walls of Jerusalem in ruins and disrepair. Verse 11 of Micah 7 was no mere promise of an urban renewal project for downtown Jerusalem, but a promise that God would silence in a big way the jeers of the tormentors who depicted God as non-existent or at least much removed from the realities of a city needing attention and fixing. But God would see to it that the walls were rebuilt as a symbol of the people once more being restored to his favor and salvation (Ps. 51:18; Isa. 60:10; Jer. 31:38–40). Note that the Hebrew word for "walls" is not the same one used for "ramparts" around the city, but rather the word used for the enclosures for vineyards and flocks.

B. *When New Boundaries Are Set.* In verse 11, the problem is to properly translate the Hebrew *hoq*, which could be rendered "a law," "a decree," "a limit," or "a boundary." Every one of the above options has been tried. C. F. Keil saw it as the "law" of Israel's exclusivity that would be abolished.[7] Carl R. Caspari viewed *hoq* as the "borders" of the land of Israel that would be extended way beyond their original compass.[8] E. W. Hengstenberg, the German Lutheran exegete, saw it differently: he said the term referred to the "decrees" imposed by the heathen rulers that would be removed. Then, Paul Kleinert concluded that this text argued for the removal of the middle "wall" of partition between Jews and Gentiles.[9]

Which is correct? It is impossible to say with any degree of finality. If it is tied to the previous verse that had just mentioned walls, perhaps this text does point to a nation with new boundaries. But whichever is true, God promises to remove every type of impediment or limiting factor for his people "in that day." For the final realization of God's work here, this text awaits God's new work in the final day of our Lord. That is when all will finally see the answer to the question, "Where is the Lord your God?"

C. *When People's Deeds Demand a Divine Response.* Verse 13 would be better rendered starting with an adversative, "but," for it describes a worldwide judgment because of the fruit of the wicked deeds of the world's inhabitants. Those who chided, "Where is the LORD your God?" will soon find out for themselves the hard way. Micah's language is very similar to that of Isaiah 11:11–16; 27:12; and Zechariah 10:8–12. Yes, the Jews of the Diaspora will return to their homeland along with some Gentiles (Isa. 2:2–5; 60:3; Zech. 14:16), but the wicked will also be dealt with by God.

II. In His Marvelous Deeds for Us (Mic. 7:14–17)

A. *Of Shepherding Us.* Micah enjoyed using the figure of a shepherd for the Good Shepherd, for he used it in all three sections of hope in his book (Mic. 2:12; 4:6–7; 7:14). This is not an unfamiliar metaphor for our Lord, for it appears rather frequently. For example, Psalm 100:3b carries it out with these words: "We are his people, the sheep of his pasture," a thought that is repeated in Psalm 95:7. Neither can one forget the great chapter in Ezekiel 34, which was the chapter Jesus alluded to when he described himself as the Good Shepherd in John 10.

The figure of the shepherd points to one who leads, guides, protects, and rules his people. Thus when Micah 7:14 depicts our Lord shepherding his people with his staff, it is not a staff used in judgment but one that functions like the rod and the staff that comfort in Psalm 23:4. This staff of the shepherd is the one used to pull back to safety a wandering sheep that had gone over the edge or fallen into a hole.

Israel is called "the flock of [his] inheritance" (v. 14) in a metaphor expressing the value and worth of the people because they were God's special possession (Exod. 19:5–6; Ps. 28:9). They were those who live by themselves "in a forest, in fertile pasturelands/Carmel" (v. 14). Indeed, Israel did live apart from the pagan nations around them, just as Balaam the prophet had prophesied in Numbers 23:9: "I see a people who live apart and do not consider themselves one of the nations." All the good grazing and farming lands, such as Carmel, Bashan, and Gilead, were in the hands of others, but the prayer to God was that these lands would be restored to Israel in the future days as they had enjoyed them in the old times. Jeremiah 50:19 had promised the same: "I will bring Israel back to his own pasture and he will graze on Carmel and Bashan; his appetite will be satisfied on the hills of Ephraim and Gilead."

B. *Of Working Miracles.* If verse 14 is a prayer, then verses 15–17 contain God's answer. Israel, and all the people of God, can expect him to intervene on their behalf, just as he had demonstrated when Israel came out of Egypt. The miracles of God were filled with his "wonders" (v. 15c), a word formed from the Hebrew root *pele'*, "wonderful," just like God's name in Isaiah 9:6 or the question asked in Jeremiah 32:27, "Is anything *too hard* for me?" God specializes in doing that which others think is difficult, too hard, or too wonderful. One of these days, God is going to demonstrate his power and wonder-working skills for Israel in their return to him in a way similar to what they saw when they left Egypt.

When the pagan nations observe the wondrous working of God on behalf of Israel, they "will see and be ashamed"; in fact, "they will lay their hands on their mouths and their ears will become deaf" (v. 16). So humiliated will these nations be that they will have no more to say or spout off about. As in Isaiah 52:15, "kings will shut their mouths" when they see the LORD in that final day moving majestically to wrap up history.

C. *Of Conquering Nations.* The conquest over the nations will be complete, for "they will lick dust like a snake" (Mic. 7:17). Not only is this metaphor still used of conquering an enemy, whether on the athletic field or the battlefield (cf. Ps. 44:25; Isa. 49:23), but it also reminds us of the first announcement of the gospel in Genesis 3:15. Both in Genesis 3:15 and here, the Hebrew article is used with the word for "serpent" or "snake." Therefore, the reference is to "the Serpent" (yes, capitalized), that old dragon, the devil, for he was, and still is, the enemy of God and his people.

However, there still remains a day to come when the nations will come "trembling out of their dens; they will turn in fear to the LORD our God" (v. 17cd). This victory of our Lord in the final day resembles the earlier victories of David, who was in the messianic line. Psalm 18:45 describes David's victory: "They all lose heart; they come trembling from their strongholds." And so they will in that final day as well, for great will be the day of our Lord!

III. In His Forgiveness of Our Sins (Mic. 7:18–20)

A. *Based on Who He Is.* The final evidence of the majesty of our Lord is seen in this section, which really is at the heart of this passage. It forms a doxology that easily compares to those found in Romans 11:33–36; Psalm 104:31–35; and Psalm 68:32–35. Here is another grand climax to a grand message of hope.

The preeminent question is, "Who is a God like you?" (v. 18). This question is embedded in the very name of Micah, for it too means, "Who is like/compares to Yah[weh]?" Over and over again we have seen the doctrine of the incomparability of the Lord stressed in these passages. Of course, it is a rhetorical question, for the answer expected is that there is no one who even comes close to comparing to our Lord. Ever since the enormous deliverance of Israel at the Red Sea, the people have sung, "Who among the gods is like you, O LORD? Who is like you—majestic in holiness, awesome in glory, working wonders?" (Exod. 15:11).

If God is great beyond all comparison, why are we so terrified by all the different problems and issues of our day? Should we not be encouraged by all the promises of God rather than being intimidated by all the empty masks of our time? If God so exceeds everyone else, what do we have to fear?

More than that, our God "pardons sin and forgives the transgression" (v. 18b). This echoes Exodus 34:5–7, for the formula for forgiveness is quite ancient. As already noted above, the literal meaning of "pardon" is a "lifting up" of the burden and weight of sin that holds us down. The literal meaning of "forgiving" here is a "passing over," an allusion to Passover night when the death angel "passed over" those houses that had applied the blood of the slain lamb to the lintels and doorposts of their homes. But even more startling is the fact that our Lord became the Paschal Lamb as the substitute for our sins, thereby making it possible for him to offer us a full release from them. That is why he does "not stay angry forever" (v. 18d). Instead, he delights to show his "mercy," a word that reflects one of the most beautiful words in the Old Testament. It appears two hundred forty-eight times and has the basic idea of "grace" extended to those the Lord chooses to favor. Translators have tried to find one, two, or even three English words that will approximate the meaning of the Hebrew *hesed*, but they have been unsuccessful. I think "grace" comes as close as any word, while many try "loving-kindness," "mercy," "covenantal love," or the like. God does not hold a grudge or store up his anger forever. No, instead, as the psalmist taught in Psalm 103:9–10, "He will not always accuse, nor will he harbor his anger forever; he does not treat us as our sins deserve or repay us according to our iniquities." So if we want to glory, or boast about anything at all, let it be in this manner: "Let him who boasts boast about this: that he understands and knows me, that I am the LORD, who exercises kindness, justice and righteousness on earth, for in these I delight" (Jer. 9:24).

B. *Based on What He Has Done.* How fabulously great is the grace and forgiveness of our Lord! Just when we could have expected nothing but his wrath and anger because of our sin, he took compassion on us and hurled our sins "into the depths of the sea" (v. 19). The figure here is the same one that was used for what God did to Pharaoh's chariots: they too were "hurled into the sea" and they sank into the depths like a stone or a lead weight (Exod. 15:4, 5, 10). God will give our sins a mighty heave as well.

The final three verses of this chapter all are linked with the book of Jonah for the afternoon reading on Yom Kippur. But even before this event, orthodox Jews gather at a stream or body of fresh or living water every year on Rosh Hashanah, the Jewish New Year, for a ceremony that is called *Tashlich*. This service is named after the Hebrew word for "hurl," or "cast," in Micah's text. Symbolically, the Jewish people empty their pockets and pretend to cast into the water the sins of the previous year as Micah 7:18–20 is recited. The picture is one of God taking our sins and washing us clean as our sins are buried in the depths of the river or ocean. God not only forgives our sins, but he also remembers them no more.[10] If some think this goes against God's omniscience, then recall that our Lord deliberately chooses not to remember our sins against us anymore.

Micah closes his book with a backward glance over the promise-plan of God. This was the plan that Yahweh had given to Abraham, Isaac, and Jacob. Its contents were "grace" (Hebrew *hesed*) and "truth." This combination of "grace and truth" began in Exodus 34:5–6 but is carried over to John 1:17, where "the law through Moses was given; grace and truth in Jesus happened" (my literal translation).

So God stands behind his promise-plan, guaranteeing it by his word (Gen. 12:2–3) and by his oath (Gen. 22:16; Mic. 7:20). This is his "everlasting covenant," or his "sworn promise." How excellent! How beautiful! How magnificent is the pardoning grace of our Lord that has been part and parcel of the overarching story of the Bible from beginning to end.

Conclusions

1. Wouldn't we all like to be free of our burden of sin? There is power in the blood of the lamb.
2. The pardoning grace of our Lord exceeds all bounds of anything we have ever known. He himself has paid all our debts and freed us indeed.
3. Who then is a pardoning God like our God? No one in the past, present, or future can or will ever pardon our sins as our Lord can and will if we will but ask him for our release.

6

MAGNIFYING THE HOLY SPIRIT FROM OUR GOD

ZECHARIAH 4:1–14

Introduction

The person and work of the Holy Spirit in the Old Testament is all too frequently dismissed with some sort of statement that in that period of time he came *upon* persons for a time and then left them. This is almost always put in contrast with the New Testament teaching where the Holy Spirit brings regeneration to us in our lost estate and now *indwells* us permanently. Such a contrast of the Holy Spirit's person and work is not accurate or fair to all the biblical texts.

Still, the questions come like a flood: Was the Holy Spirit active during the Old Testament times as he was in the New? Did he regenerate persons then as he does now? Did he indwell them, fill them, seal them, and empower them as he does today?

One writer chided that all "attempts to find any evidence of revivals taking place in Bible times and recorded in Scripture . . . [were] futile. . . . Though revivals are defined as being special visitations of the Holy Spirit, this could not have happened in Old Testament times, because 'the Holy Spirit was not yet given' (John 7:39)."[1]

But the whole assertion is invalid. First of all, I have shown elsewhere that there were at least sixteen major revivals in the Old and New Testaments.[2] Moreover, even though John 7:38–39 contains some difficult verses, what is expected here is the coming of the Holy Spirit *in state* at Pentecost, just as the blessing of the new birth was experienced in the Old Testament but was applied to believers proleptically, waiting for Calvary to pay the promised redemption for our sins. The Feast of Pentecost took place fifty days after the work of Christ on the cross. The Holy Spirit did not come quietly, but as T. Goodwin said, "He must have a coming in state, in a solemn and visible manner, accompanied with visible effects as Christ had on Calvary, and whereof all the Jews should be, and were, witnesses."[3]

But even more helpful in answering this distorted assertion that the Holy Spirit came for the first time to take up permanent residence in a believer only in New Testament times was G. Smeaton's comment on John 7:37–38:

> But the apostle adds [in John 7:37–38] that "the Spirit was not yet" because Christ's glorification had not yet arrived. He does not mean that the Spirit did not yet exist—for all Scripture attests His eternal preexistence—nor that His regenerative efficacy was still unknown—for countless millions had been regenerated by His power since the first promise in Gen.—but that these operations of the Spirit had been but an anticipation of the atoning gift of Christ rather than a GIVING. The apostle speaks comparatively, not absolutely.[4]

Let us, therefore, examine some of these key texts in the context of the Old Testament times themselves.

Psalm 51:11. A central text in this discussion of the Holy Spirit's work and presence in the Old Testament is Psalm 51:11: "Do not cast me from your presence or take your Holy Spirit from me. Restore to me the joy of your salvation." Now some interpreters believe that what David is talking about here is the gift of government, which came upon him as he was anointed as king (1 Sam. 16:13–14). At the same time, it is said that the gift of the Holy Spirit was taken from King Saul so that he was no longer fit to rule the country.

But the context of Psalm 51:11 is decidedly against such a narrow interpretation of the work of the Holy Spirit in this text. Had not David just prayed (v. 10), "Create in me a pure heart, O God, and renew a steadfast spirit within me"? It was no one less than A. B. Simpson who believed that David's mention of the Holy Spirit referred to the one who "will come into the heart that has been made right, and dwell within us in His power and holiness."[5] Clearly, David wanted to continue to experience the indwelling presence of the Holy Spirit in his heart and life.

The person of the Holy Spirit does more during the Old Testament period, therefore, than merely working in creation, equipping persons for special acts or spheres of service, giving others wisdom and skill in craftsmanship or as channels of prophetic inspiration. The Holy Spirit also works in regenerating and indwelling every Old Testament believer who has ever entered into the new birth—yes, even prior to the events on Calvary. Men and women were justified by faith as a gift of God, and not by works, lest anyone (Adam, Eve, Noah, Abraham, or any other Old Testament saint) should boast (Eph. 2:5b, 9). This faith did not just pop out of nowhere, but it came as a result of the inner working of the Holy Spirit, because the Old Testament saints, like us, were regenerated and indwelt by the Holy Spirit.

John 3:1–15. In order to show that this indeed was the case, let us go to a situation that involved Rabbi Nicodemus coming to Jesus (prior to the events of Calvary, remember) to inquire about Jesus's miraculous signs (John 3:2). Our Lord immediately steered him to an even greater question: How can a person see the kingdom of God unless he or she is born again? (v. 3).

In response to that provocative announcement, Nicodemus wanted to know how people could be born a second time after they had entered this world. It all sounded so new and different. Jesus patiently explained that this new birth is accomplished by the work of the Spirit of God. Now that really halted this Pharisee in his tracks. "How can this be?" he puzzled (v. 9).

Now it was Jesus's turn to express surprise, for he wanted to know how this rabbi could have been a teacher of the Jews and yet not grasp what he was being told from the Old Testament texts (v. 10).

Had Nicodemus never read or taught from Ezekiel 36:25–32 about the "new heart" and the "new Spirit?" How could he have missed this truth?

My point in appealing to this passage in John 3 is not to settle doctrine for the Old Testament by appealing to the New Testament (a move we generally rebuke as a form of eisegesis) but to show that our Lord, even prior to the events surrounding his death, burial, and resurrection, thought it was altogether reasonable for a person to experience being "born again" by means of the regenerating work of the Holy Spirit. And teachers who functioned with only the Old Testament as their source of religious authority should likewise have been alert to this same teaching and ready to share it with others.

Isaiah 63:7–14. This text shares with Psalm 51:11 the distinction of being the only other place in the Old Testament where—three times, in fact—the full name of the "Holy Spirit" occurs. In this hymn, Israel remembers what the Holy Spirit accomplished in their history. The text begins with Israel praising God for his kindness and goodness. It recalls how God showed his "love" and "mercy" (v. 9) during the exodus and the wilderness experience. Yet verse 10 shows how Israel "rebelled" and "grieved" God's Holy Spirit during those same days as Israel challenged the authority of Yahweh. The same parallelism of "rebelling" and "grieving" the Holy Spirit is found in Psalm 78:40, where Israel expressed that same attitude, not to the Holy Spirit, this time, but to Yahweh—"How often they rebelled against him [Yahweh] in the desert and grieved him [Yahweh] in the wasteland."[6] The comparison of these two texts (Isa. 63:10 and Ps. 78:40) shows that grieving and rebelling against the Holy Spirit is the same as grieving and rebelling against Yahweh. Mr. Choi, one of my ThM students, points out that the same parallelism is found in Isaiah 63:14, which affirms, "Like cattle that go down to the plain, they [the Israelites] were given rest by the Spirit of the LORD. This is how you [Yahweh] guided your people to make for yourself a glorious name." Thus, from the Hebrew parallelism, it is clear that the Spirit of the LORD who caused Israel to rest was also closely identified with the work Yahweh effected as he led his people during the Old Testament times.

Ezekiel 36:24–28. This is the text that our Lord Jesus must have had in mind as he held Nicodemus accountable for teaching about the new birth and the work of the Holy Spirit. It reads: "I will give you a new heart and put a new spirit in you; I will remove from you your heart of stone and give you a heart of flesh. And I will put my Spirit in you and move you to follow my decrees and be careful to keep my laws" (vv. 26–27).

Who else but the Holy Spirit could so touch, change, transform, and indwell the inner being of a human that the person could be changed from possessing a heart of stone and a heart of flesh to acquiring a new heart and a new Spirit? Is this not what Paul also taught in Romans 2:29: "No, a man is a Jew [only] if he is one inwardly; and circumcision is circumcision of the heart, by the Spirit." The Holy Spirit was the same operator on the heart both in the Old and New Testaments.

It is this linkage, the association of the Holy Spirit with the radical inner heart transformation (here called the "circumcision of the heart"), that opens up the way for seeing similar works of the Holy Spirit in both testaments. This is the same point that Jesus was making in John 3:3–8: it is the Spirit who performs that basic transformation and regeneration of the heart on all who believe. It is the metaphor of the "circumcision of the heart" that points to a fundamental interior renovation of the most interior part of a person. Thus the Old Testament saint not only was regenerated, but also personally experienced the transforming power of God in all its fullness. The Holy Spirit was involved in each person's new birth prior to the cross of Christ, according to Ezekiel 36:24–28.[7]

Joel 2:28–32. The last passage we will consider in this short survey of key evidence for the Holy Spirit's work and presence in the Old Testament is Joel 2:28–32. An invasion of four waves of locusts was enough to devastate the land of Judah during Joel's day. But as a result of his preaching, the people did repent, as the four past-tense verbs in Joel 2:28 clearly indicate.[8]

The immediate effect was a return to production of the fields and pastures (Joel 2:19–27), which came "at the first" (Hebrew literal translation of Joel 2:23d). There was not only a "now" in this typical inaugurated eschatology, but also a future "then," "afterward" (v. 28), or "after this." Thus, whereas showers had come to green up the pastures and to bring new crops to harvest as the first and immediate response to repentance and renewal, God would yet send a veritable "downpour" of his Holy Spirit in a last day, especially in the day of the Lord. In those "latter days," the Holy Spirit would pour out his Spirit on "all people," regardless of sex ("sons and daughters"), age ("old men" and "young men"), or even race ("my servants," who were always Gentiles in Jewish households). Later, on the day of Pentecost, Peter said that what people were witnessing that day was at least a part of what Joel had predicted (Acts 2:16).

It is impossible to avoid the presence and work of the Holy Spirit in the Old Testament. It is this teaching that helps us as we approach a text like Zechariah 4:1–14. No wonder it is altogether proper to "Magnify the Holy Spirit from Our God" in the first thirty-nine books of the Bible.

An Exposition of Zechariah 4:1–14

Easily, the central idea, or focal point, of this chapter is verse 6b: "This is the word of the Lord to Zerubbabel, 'Not by might nor by power, but by my Spirit,' says the Lord Almighty." The question then is this: "How?" How can we magnify the Holy Spirit from our God? The answer is by noting three key "observations" (our homiletical key word) that are found in Zechariah 4:1–14. These three observations are:

I. God's Work Is Accomplished by God's Spirit (Zech. 4:1–6)
II. God's Work Must Not Be Despised for Its Small Beginnings (Zech. 4:7–10)
III. God's Work Values People More Than Institutions (Zech. 4:11–14)

The prophet Zechariah was given eight night visions in Zechariah 1:7–6:8. In more ways than one, the fourth vision (3:1–10, a vision of the high priest Joshua standing in his filthy, dung-spattered garments and being given new, rich garments, representing Israel's sins being removed in a single day) and the fifth vision (4:1–14, a vision of a gold lampstand and the two olive trees) are central to the eight visions. Perhaps a brief retrospective look at the preceding four visions will better set the stage for understanding what is involved in the fifth of these eight visions.

God wanted to convey through these symbolic prophecies a word that was "kind and comforting" (Zech. 1:13) in its assurance to the people. Despite their seventy years in captivity in Babylon and their return to the land sixteen years before (it was now 520 BC), God wanted to assure his people that he had neither forsaken them forever nor cast them off from being his people. True, Israel had experienced the oppressive bondage of such Gentile world powers as Assyria and Babylon, but the "angel of the LORD" was still pleading their case for them (1:8–12). This "angel," who was no less than Yahweh himself, was far from being merely indifferent to this nation and its people, for he was exceedingly angry (1:14–15) with the nations that had touched Israel, the "apple of his eye" (2:8). Even though these Gentile nations and empire-powers had raised their horns to scatter "Judah, Israel and Jerusalem" (1:18–21), God promised that these "horns" (national powers) would themselves be broken and "thrown down." However, the city of Jerusalem would be rebuilt and God himself would be a "wall of fire around it" (2:5), revealing his "glory within" (2:5).

This promise was not limited to Jerusalem. The whole land would sense the same blessing of God as the multitude of people and possessions spilled out across the countryside (2:4). Best of all, God himself would live among them (2:10). Moreover, many nationalities would be represented as the nations joined themselves to the Lord (2:11), just as the Abrahamic promise had foretold.

All of this seemed too good to be true, for had not Israel and Judah sinned grievously and had not their moral defilement reached unprecedented heights? Was this not enough for them to forfeit their place as the people of God?

The answer to this very logical question was given in the fourth vision, one of the two central visions of the eight. Zechariah 3:1–10 pictures Joshua, the high priest of that day, representing all the people and their sin, for he is depicted in filthy, perhaps dung-spattered clothes (3:3). But even if the high priest, like our Lord, bears the sin of all the people (depicted in his soiled robe), yet the Lord will remove all that moral filth from the daughter of Zion "in a single day" (3:9). One day the Jewish people are going to have their eyes opened to recognize that Jesus the Messiah gave his life as the atoning work of God for all who would receive his cleansing.

This one, who is called "the Branch" (3:8), and "my servant" (3:8) will come in "rich garments" (3:4) of the festal dress of the priesthood with the high priestly miter on his head bearing a plate inscribed with this wording: "Holiness to Yahweh."

Israel will be equipped not only to have fellowship with the Lord, now that they are cleansed, but also to fulfill the ancient mission given to them since the days of the Abrahamic covenant in Genesis 12:3: "All peoples on earth will be blessed through you." Now they will be a blessing and a light to the nations of the earth. Now we are ready for the fifth vision, the parallel central vision, which sees Israel deployed as disseminators of the light of God to the world.

I. God's Work Is Accomplished by God's Spirit (Zech. 4:1-6)

Some suggest a brief respite from the previous four visions before the angel returned to ask Zechariah once again, "What do you see?" (4:1). Be that as it may, after being awakened to a spiritually heightened state once again, the prophet is shown "a solid golden lampstand, with a bowl at the top and seven lights on it, with seven channels [pipes] to the lights" (4:2).[9]

It must be noted that this is not the same lampstand as the seven-branched menorah depicted on Titus's Arch in Rome as part of the booty taken by the Roman armies. Instead, it was a sort of cylindrical pedestal with, or forming, a bowl on top. The bowl had seven spouts. If this was anything like the seven-pinched pottery lamps from about 900 BC found in Israel at both Dan and Dothan, then what is described here is a saucer-shaped lamp on a stand that has seven pinches, or spouts, with wicks lying in the pinches so that one end lies in the saucer absorbing oil by the processes of convection and the other end is the wick with a flame burning the oil. There are also two olive trees standing, one to the right and the other to the left of the bowl.

Concerning all of this symbolism, the prophet asks three times (4:4, 11, 12), "What are these?" The angel asks, "Do you not know what these are?" (4:5). "No," answers the prophet. The prophet's obtuseness has been a boon to later interpreters, for it saves multiple theories about what each of these things meant!

Instead of answering immediately, the interpreting angel gives the prophet a word that is to be an encouragement to Zerubbabel as leader of this disheartened people. That word was: " 'Not by might nor by power, but by my Spirit,' says the LORD Almighty" (4:6). I believe it was J. Vernon McGee who suggested a more colloquial rendering: " 'Nor by brawn nor by brain, but by my Spirit,' says the LORD of Hosts." Nevertheless, the point is clear: any work that the returnees or their leaders were going to accomplish would happen only through the power of the Holy Spirit. It was just plain worthless to rely on human resources, on human sagacity, or on human strength.

Had the people not remembered the fiasco of sixteen years earlier when the returnees first saw the ruins of the temple and started to lay the foundations for it in their own strength, only to have discouragement set in? A great tumult arose over whether the temple footprint as seen in its footers was too small and too unlike what Solomon's temple had been (Ezra 3:8–13). Human effort, without the supply of the ministry of the Holy Spirit (or in the symbolism of this vision, the oil) quickly burns itself out.

The oil of the Holy Spirit is exactly what is needed for the work and evidence of the presence of God, for the work of God done by the Holy Spirit of God will never lack God's provision, God's presence, or his power. Resist or elevate another principle in place of this one, and we will learn the hard way that the oil of the Holy Spirit cannot be substituted for or disposed of for doing the work of God.

The word for "might" (Hebrew *hayil*) also means an "army" or "host," and represented the strength and resources of many. The word for "power" (Hebrew *koah*) usually represented the human strength of a single individual. When taken together, the two words point to all types of human strength—physical, mental, moral, and psychological.

So what is the caution raised here for all believers? It is that God's work cannot be accomplished by our resoluteness alone, be those resolutions ever so high, so pure, and so filled with positive motivations. Insofar as they are purely of a human nature, they cannot eventuate in the work God wants to see us do. Why then does the church of God or the missionary movement evidence major flaws and inadequacies? Probably a good part of the reason is because we are so much in danger of imagining that all this work of God can be done by our own abilities and resoluteness. God's work must be done by a total dependence on the Holy Spirit, or it will always fall short, lacking God's provision and God's power.

Thus far we have spoken about these two olive trees representing the governor and the high priest (Zerubbabel and Joshua), who needed to be encouraged as leaders on how to go about doing tasks that seemed to be mind-boggling in their day, and in our day as well. But now we must ask, "What about the lampstand?" Surely it typified the high calling of God for Israel to be a light to the nations around them. That was the calling the people of Abraham's line received in Ur of the Chaldees in Genesis 12:3. This was missionary fervor at its highest and best. There was no need to wait for the Great Commission in Matthew and Mark's Gospels.

God eventually did remove the *scepter* of government from Israel, but in his long-suffering and kindness, he never removed her calling to be a *candlestick* and a *lampstand* for the Lord. That stood as a symbol of Israel's religious and national calling to be a witness for God to everyone worldwide. Only when the nation's cup of iniquity was filled was the kingdom of God temporarily removed and given to a people bringing forth the fruit thereof.

The wicks, therefore, represent the people who are to minister the flame and light of the truth to all. Some connect this to the seven golden lampstands of Revelation 1:12, seeing those as representing the ones who take up the slack left by Israel in the meantime. Surely in that New Testament setting the seven lamps are the seven churches of Asia Minor (present-day Turkey); but rather than being direct fulfillments of Zechariah's prophecy, they seem to have illustrative significance.

Let us now turn to the next observation to find the message and interpretation embodied in the text that will help us regard these symbols and emblems.

II. God's Work Must Not Be Despised for Its Small Beginnings (Zech. 4:7-10)

The principle announced in verse 6 is applied and explained in verse 7. The "mighty mountain" was a metaphor for the colossal set of obstacles that stood in the way of rebuilding the temple. Verse 9 says that the hands of Zerubbabel "have laid the foundation of this temple; his hands will also complete it." Indeed, this prophecy was fulfilled, but it was some four years after the prophets Haggai and Zechariah predicted it in the "second year of King Darius" (Hag. 1:1; cf. Zech. 1:1), or 520 BC. It was not until the "sixth year of the reign of King Darius," on the "third day of the month Adar" (Ezra 6:14–15), that the temple was finally finished.

But this word about a "mighty mountain" applied to more than the mere building of the temple. In the Jewish Targum, Rabbi Kimchi, as did a number of Christian interpreters, applied it also to the restoration of the kingdom of God in the face of the "mountain" of the Gentile world powers. One day, even those colossal impediments that seem like mountains right now will be removed and also become "a plain," or "level ground" (4:7).

To many at that time, one of the chief causes for such slow progress on the house of God must have been that many saw this as too insignificant and as a work of "small things" (4:10). Haggai had tried to mitigate this corrosive spirit in their midst in Haggai 2:3: "Who of you is left who saw this house in its former glory? How does it look to you now? Does it not seem to you like nothing?" But if it is in the will of God and is connected to the plan he is working for all ages and times, what may appear to be insignificant in our eyes actually is of enormous significance. It is directly connected to the great work of our Lord in his consummation in that final day of all things. That is what Haggai the prophet taught in Haggai 2:6–9.

God's work and plan rested, in this case, on the "plumb line" (literally "stone of tin" in Hebrew) in the hand of Zerubbabel (4:10). Some render this plummet as a "Chosen Stone" (Jerusalem Bible), while others render it a "stone of Separation." The seven ("seven," because of God's completeness?) eyes are those of God's special providence that "range throughout the earth to strengthen those whose hearts are fully committed to him" (2 Chron. 16:9).

So let us stop belittling and demeaning what we may think of as small works, for if they are ordained of God, his omniscient presence inspects what goes on until it is finished; it is linked with the grand design that our Lord has for all that is taking place in heaven and on earth. There are no "small potatoes" in God's work, which is done by his Holy Spirit; it will blossom and flourish gloriously, because it is linked with God's final triumph in that final day.

"Then he will bring out the capstone to shouts of 'God bless it! God bless it!'" (v. 7). This stone was the topping out or capping stone that was wedged into place as the final stone in the project. It had been set aside for the unique place (usually in the arch) it would finally have in the temple, just as Jesus was the special stone marked precisely for the unique role he would play in our salvation. The joy expressed is to acknowledge that God has done it all. Here is the proof that God has sent Haggai, Zechariah, Zerubbabel, and Joshua. They began and they finished what God had tasked them with doing.

III. God's Work Values People More Than Institutions (Zech. 4:11–14)

The prophet does not remain preoccupied with the building, important as it may be; people are more than mere props in the work of God. They are "anointed" (4:14) and set apart for the tasks God has given to them as his representatives.

Certainly the temple needed the golden lampstand and the lampstand needed the fuel of the Holy Spirit to illuminate the temple and to serve as a symbol of the light of the gospel that was to be shown around the world. But the high priest Joshua and the governor Zerubbabel were right there alongside this lampstand as God's instruments to be used for his glory.

It seems that God has always been pleased to use people; an institution by itself does not appear to be enough to transform the world. People are needed if the light of the gospel is to be displayed throughout the whole earth. This is not to cast a vote only for the laity or only for the leaders; both are needed.

Some have said, with what must be a degree of pretentiousness, that God will do what he wants to do without any help from any of us, thank you. But this can only be seen as a cop-out and a shirking of our duties. God loves people, and he works with and through people to the degree that we will let him do so. Therefore, what we need are a few good men and a few good women energized by the Holy Spirit to do great exploits for our God.

Conclusions

1. The Holy Spirit is central to all works or missions that we wish to do or see done for the Lord.
2. If this is so, then we must not "grieve the Holy Spirit" (Eph. 4:30) or "quench the Spirit" (1 Thess. 5:19 NASB), but rather we must "walk in the Spirit" (Gal. 5:16 KJV).
3. God will use mortals as his chosen instruments by which he will fire up his church (lampstand) and his lamps (the laity and leaders) through the Holy Spirit.
4. We must stop judging negatively any work of God that appears for the moment to be small, for it is formed according to the principle of "not by might nor by power, but by my Spirit," and it will not only last but also be directly connected and linked with what God is going to do in the last day.

7

MAGNIFYING THE AWESOME
CHARACTER OF OUR GOD

PSALM 139:1–18

Introduction

Psalm 139:1–18 reveals three of the characteristics of our Lord that far transcend anything we mortals ever have or could experience. Those three attributes, qualities, or characteristics are: his omniscience, his omnipresence, and his omnipotence. This has to be one of the greatest teaching, or "chair," passages in the Bible where all three of these most important characteristics of our Lord can be found together.

Prior to examining the teaching or preaching text from this psalm itself, let us focus on the whole topic of the attributes or characteristics of God, and let us do so through the lens of systematic theology. Often in our day, this discipline is avoided, or regarded as the weak sister in the study of theology. However, we leave behind what this discipline has to offer at our own peril; to do so would reduce the insights that our preaching might more strategically embrace, even in its expository forms. Therefore, let us look at these three qualities of our God from the standpoint of systematic theology. These attributes make it especially possible for us to better know the essence and nature of God himself and to differentiate him from all other competitors in the universe. So superlative are all qualities and attributes of our God that church theologians have almost exhausted themselves suggesting one scheme after another in order to classify all these divine attributes. But ultimately the theologians end up disagreeing with each other as to which divine quality goes under which rubric. Attempts to classify and categorize the divine characteristics do not seem to have reached a consensus and have not proved ultimately to be all that helpful. Therefore, I do not think it worthwhile, or helpful to the body of Christ, to belabor any of those schemes. Instead, we will proceed directly to a discussion of each of these three characteristics as introduced by Psalm 139.

Omniscience[1]

First of all, let it be fairly stated that there are no words in the Bible, in either Hebrew or Greek, that could be rendered into English (or any other language) as "omniscience." This word, instead, represents our attempt to gather up all the teaching of the Bible on what it says that God knows. Nevertheless the meaning of this word is fairly straightforward: it is God's ability to know everything, not in a detached, abstract, or speculative way, but rather a knowing that comes from genuine experience, wherein one knows intimately and totally in a way that far surpasses human modes of knowledge. This knowledge, which is a great comfort to God's people, is simultaneously a cause for great concern and alarm to all the unrighteous, for there is nothing that remains hidden or outside the sphere of God's knowledge.

To begin our study, we must note that God's knowledge is so all-encompassing that he knows not only specific things, but also what could have happened, even if it never takes place. For example, in 1 Samuel 23, David has just rescued the city of Keilah from the Philistines at the direction of God, even while he was still being pursued by King Saul. But when David learned that Saul was intent on capturing him while he was still in Keilah, David asked God for direction. He asked the Lord two questions: will Saul march down here in an attempt to capture me in this city? and will the people I have just delivered from the Philistines ungratefully hand me over to King Saul if I stay here? The answer to both questions was, "Yes." Obviously David got out of Keilah quickly. But note that God told David both what did happen (in the case of Saul's actions) and what might or could have happened as well (in the case of the people possibly handing David over to King Saul).

The same type of alternative prospect is found in Jeremiah 38:17–23. Here the prophet, speaking on behalf of the God of heaven, outlines for King Zedekiah two alternative responses he could make in light of the threatening situation that the Babylonian king Nebuchadnezzar presented, along with what would happen if he chose one course of action or the other. God knows not only the what-will-happen scenarios, but also the what-if scenarios.

Jesus demonstrates that same quality of omniscience for both what does happen and what could happen. Jesus said in Matthew 11:21, "Woe to you, Korazin! Woe to you, Bethsaida! If the miracles that were performed in you had been performed in Tyre and Sidon, they would have repented long ago in sackcloth and ashes."

God not only knows the actual and possible happenings, but his knowledge also is complete and total, just as Elihu taught: "One perfect in knowledge is with you" (Job 36:4; cf. 37:16). The writer of Hebrews (4:13) put it even more succinctly: "Nothing in all creation is hidden from God's sight. Everything is uncovered and laid bare before the eyes of him to whom we must give account." This is why God does not need anyone to teach him knowledge (Job 21:22; Isa. 40:14).

Even more intricate is the extent of the knowledge of our Lord. He created the whole physical universe by his wisdom, and thus the cosmos functions in accordance with the design he implanted in the whole created order (Ps. 104:19; 147:4–5). His knowledge also covers each individual and all the specifics of each person's life (Ps. 33:13–15). Psalm 139:1–4 emphasizes the truth that God knows everything there is to know about each mortal and there is nothing that can happen to us that will catch God off guard or by surprise.

He even keeps track of our tears (Ps. 56:8) and the number of hairs on our heads (Matt. 10:30). Add to that the announcement that God knows our innermost thoughts and our hearts, so there is no use trying to hide anything from him (Ps. 139:2; Prov. 24:12; Isa. 29:15; 40:27–28; Acts 15:8). God's omniscience covers all that is to be known, including all future events. He knew exactly what Cyrus would be named and what he would do two centuries or more before he was born (Isa. 44:28). God's knowledge and wisdom are awesome and magnificent indeed.

Some are quick to raise objections to such a high view of God's omniscience. For example: "If God knows everything, how is it that he can remove my sin from his memory when I confess it to him, thereby forgiving me and remembering it against me no more?" The answer is that God chooses not to count these sins *against* me anymore or to bring them to mind every time he thinks of me.

Another quickly objects, "Yes, but if God is incorporeal, how can he have experiential knowledge, since we agree he does not have any of the five senses that mortals have?" Again the answer is that there is a difference between propositional knowledge (about facts) and relational or experiential knowledge. One can accurately describe in propositions experiences one has never had personally. It is not always necessary for one to experience pain, feel heat, smell something putrid, or the like, in order to know what the person experiencing it is talking about. If the experience of the sensation is separate from acquiring knowledge about it, then God can surely have informational content about all sorts of experiences without personally experiencing them himself in a corporeal setting.

Omnipresence[2]

Some theologians use the term "immensity" as a synonym for God's omnipresence. Here we speak of God's infinity in relation to space, thereby signifying that God is present in all his being at each point in space without projecting one part of him at one place and another part of him at another point in space.

Once again, there are no direct biblical terms that translate exactly into what our words *immensity* or *omnipresence* stand for, but that does not mean that the concepts are missing. Did not Jeremiah (23:23–24) teach this very truth? He wrote, "'Am I only a God nearby?' declares the LORD, 'and not a God far away? Can anyone hide in secret places so that I cannot see him?' declares the LORD. 'Do not I fill heaven and earth?' declares the LORD." The same truth is also laid out plainly in Psalm 139:7–12, which we will look at a little later in this chapter. And surely Jonah learned that even by going into the bowels of the sea he could not escape from the presence of God (Jon. 1:3). Solomon also announced the same truth as the temple was being dedicated. God could not be contained in a building, even if it were the temple itself, for if the heavens, and even the highest heavens, could not contain him, what chance did a temple have (1 Kings 8:27; cf. Isa. 66:1)? Moreover, as Stephen noted, God does not dwell in temples made with hands (Acts 7:48–49).

In addition to God's ontological presence, he was also present with his people spiritually. In the days of King Jehoahaz of Israel, God turned back the oppression of the Syrian king Hazael, noting that he would not cast his people away from his presence (2 Kings 13:23). In the New Testament, Jesus promised that where two or three are gathered together in his name, there he is in their midst (Matt. 18:20). Moreover, as the believers went forth to witness to every nation, Jesus promised that he would be with them, even to the end of the age (Matt. 28:19–20; Acts 1:8).

Despite the comfort that this attribute brings to the believer, there are still areas of confusion in the minds of some objectors. They want to know, "If God is present everywhere, does that mean he is also in hell?" Surprisingly, the answer is "Yes." God is ontologically present everywhere, even in hell, but he is not *ethically* present with unbelievers, nor does it mean that hell's inhabitants are aware of his presence or have any relationship with him.

Again some object: "If God is without a body, how can he fill any space, not to mention all spaces at one time?" The answer again is that God is present ontologically (in his being), but not physically. This should be no harder to grasp than the fact that our immaterial human minds take up no space, but are still present with the ones to whom the minds belong. In a similar manner, God is completely immaterial, yet he is everywhere present at once along with or at each point in space. We do not say that God is present ontologically *as* each point in space, for that would lead us to pantheism. He is present *with* every point in space, but not *as* each point. To say otherwise would be to make everything divine, which is pantheism.

One last objection queries: "How can God come down to a place if he is already present everywhere, or how can Christ or the Holy Spirit indwell believers if God is everywhere present?" The answer is that his "coming down," as in his investigation of the Tower of Babel (Gen. 11:5–7) or Sodom and Gomorrah (Gen. 18:2), or in sending his Son into the world (John 4:34; 10:30), is best understood as anthropomorphic language that stresses the focusing of the divine intention on a special act, or as a manifestation or emphasis for a special intention that in no way detracts from his continued presence everywhere.

God also indwells believers in a spiritual way that is not true of unbelievers, but he is not present in believers in the same way that he is present in the incarnate Christ. For Christ's very being (or that of the Holy Spirit) does not take over our being or become a new entity added to our human nature so that we are thereby deified. Rather, God has a spiritual relationship with his own people, and he is present with them morally and ethically.

No wonder, then, the psalmist asks: "Where can I flee from your presence?" (Ps. 139:7). The answer is: "Nowhere!"

Omnipotence[3]

Unless we count *El Shaddai*, which means "God Almighty," as an equivalent Hebrew word for omnipotence, there is no Hebrew word that comes close to our rubric of omnipotence. However, there is a Greek word, *pantokrator*, which comes from *pas*, "all," and *kratos*, meaning "power." *Pantokrator* is used in the New Testament book of Revelation exclusively in reference to God (Rev. 1:8; 4:8; 11:17; 15:3; 16:7, 14; 19:6, 15; 21:22). Elsewhere in both testaments the concept is represented by numerous words and concepts.

Defining the concept of God's omnipotence is not as simple as it might appear at first. Some give up on the term *omnipotence* and simply affirm that God is "almighty" and that his power goes way beyond that of any other being. There is, in this case, no need for the term *omnipotence*.

Omnipotence is generally understood to mean that God has power to do what he wants or needs to do so long as it is not logically contradictory and so long as it is done within his moral perfections. The biblical evidence supports such a view: "Power belongs to God" (Ps. 62:11 my translation). The prophet Isaiah calls God "the Mighty One of Israel" (Isa. 1:24). The psalmist (Ps. 106:2) asks, "Who can proclaim the mighty acts of the LORD?" Was it not the Lord himself who brought Israel out of Egypt with his great power (Exod. 32:11; Deut. 4:34; 5:15; 6:21; 7:8, 19; 9:26, 29; 26:8) and his great arm?

God's power can be seen not only in his physical deeds of deliverance and intervention, but also in his work of saving individuals from their sin (Matt. 19:25–26). What seems impossible from a human standpoint is more than possible with God. From God the Father and Jesus also came power given to the disciples to perform miracles (Matt. 10:1; Mark 6:7; Luke 10:19). Jesus also raised Lazarus from the dead by the same divine power (John 11:43–44).

Finally, at the return of our Lord there will be an enormous display of the power of God as the kingdom of God irrupts on earth (Matt. 24:30; Mark 13:26; Luke 21:27). Surely our God is great in his power and deeds.

Why, then, do some object to the term *omnipotence* or have trouble defining it? It is because some pit the power of God against logical contradictions or against some of his other attributes. They ask in a silly manner, "Can God make ropes with only one end?" "Can God make round squares or rocks that he cannot lift?" "Can God change the past, or can he create another God?"

In answer to these questions, we note that some carelessly affirm that God's power is absolute, with no restrictions or qualifications. To be sure, some biblical passages at first glance would seem to suggest that notion. Job affirmed: "I know that you can do all things; no plan of yours can be thwarted" (Job 42:2). Indeed, nothing is too hard for the LORD (Gen. 18:14). This is all true, but we must not define omnipotence so as to allow God to do what is actually contradictory. Theonomists generally argue that God's power is absolute and there are no limitations on it. But, as we will see, there is no need to raise God's power to an absolute level at the expense of some of his other perfections or moral and ethical considerations.

Others (e.g., Open Theism) go to the opposite point of view and claim that God's power is finite and limited. This is their way of trying to solve the problem of evil, but in this view, God's goodness is upheld at the expense of his power. Surely Scripture does not support this definition of omnipotence either.

The best way to define omnipotence is to teach and preach that God has all power and every power, but power that is logically consistent and that shows his moral perfection in all his other attributes as well. One cannot pit his power and might against what is logically possible or against his moral attributes such as his holiness, justice, truth, and love. Thus, God cannot (and does not): (1) do what is logically contradictory, (2) alter the past, (3) cause the free acts of other agents, or (4) do evil or sin.

An Exposition of Psalm 139:1–18

The focal point, or big idea, of this text is found in verses 17–18: "How precious to me are your thoughts, O God! How vast is the sum of them! Were I to count them, they would outnumber the grains of sand." The works, plans, thoughts, and character of God himself are so overwhelming that the psalmist calls them "precious," or as we would say, they are "wonderful," or just plain "mind-boggling." It is from this pivot point that we derive our subject, "Magnifying the Awesome Character of Our God."

This psalm exhibits a structure of four equal strophes containing six verses each. For our purposes here, we will consider only the first three of these sections: verses 1–6, 7–12, and 13–18.

When I applied the six interrogatives to this text (Who? What? Why? Where? When? and How?), I decided that the question answered in the focal point and our subject was *What?* That led me to the homiletical key word of "characteristics." Since there are three strophes, my transitional sentence is: There are *three characteristics* of our God that magnify his awesomeness to us. They are:

I. Our God Is Omniscient (Ps. 139:1–6)
II. Our God Is Omnipresent (Ps. 139:7–12)
III. Our God Is Omnipotent (Ps. 139:13–18)

I. Our God Is Omniscient (Ps. 139:1–6)

Steve Roy conducted a comprehensive survey of the Bible on divine foreknowledge and concluded that there are 164 texts that explicitly teach or affirm God's foreknowledge. In addition to these 164 texts, there are another 271 texts that teach or affirm other aspects of God's omniscience (either of past, present, or possible aspects of knowing) and another 128 texts that describe what God will do through nature. In 1,893 texts, Roy continues, the Bible tells what God will do in and through human beings.[4]

It is clear from the opening words of this psalm that our Lord knows all about each of us; we are known thoroughly. So extensive and intensive has been God's examination of each of us that the text uses the word "searched." The same word is used of "spying" out a land (Judg. 18:2), of "investigating" a case (Deut. 13:14), of "digging" for precious stones (Job 28:3), and of the "penetrating look" of the Lord into our hearts (Jer. 17:10). To use a colloquial phrase for a moment, the Lord really "digs" us, only here it is used of his probing, reconnoitering, and investigating of all of us and all our ways.

God knows the totality of our acts, whether we are traveling, resting, starting out on a journey, or returning from one (v. 3). God "discerns," or literally "sifts," or "winnows" all of our life's actions so that he is intimately acquainted with all of them (v. 3).

Even my thoughts and my intentions (v. 4a) are fully known by the Lord, for he knows even "before a word is on my tongue" what it will be. Mortals do not always know what they are going to say, but God knows even before we begin to speak. Even more startling is the fact that our Lord "know[s] it completely" (v. 4b) and in its entirety! Think of all the possible thoughts that pass through our minds: thoughts of jealousy, hatred, anger, cheating, lying, and the like. Fortunately, other persons cannot read our minds and see just what is stored up there, but God in his omniscience knows it all even before we utter the words.

The psalmist continues: "You hem me in, behind and before" (v. 5a). There can be no escaping or fleeing from God, no matter how desperate our circumstances. God has "laid [his] hand [on us] (v. 5b) so that there is no escaping. The hand of God can be heavy (Job 23:2) upon us, or his hand can rest on us and on our adversary as the hand of an arbitrator or reconciler (Job 9:33). But in any event, with God's hand on us, we are completely in his power.

All such thoughts about the greatness, immensity, and incomprehensibility of God and his knowledge of everything are just plain awesome, declares the psalmist: "[It] is too wonderful for me, too lofty for me to attain" (v. 6). The Hebrew word for "wonderful" is the root *pele'*, meaning it is too "extraordinary," too "marvelous," beyond anything we can think or imagine. Mortals never have comprehensive or exhaustive knowledge with an absolute penetration or understanding of any object or subject, but God's understanding is infinite and complete. Like David, we can have adequate knowledge on many subjects, but also like David, we do not have anything like comprehensive knowledge.

II. Our God Is Omnipresent (Ps. 139:7–12)

Once again, instead of offering a general statement about the being of God, David relates God's omnipresence to some specifics. He relates the presence of God to the Holy Spirit, just as John's Gospel does in John 14:16: "And I will ask the Father, and he will give you another Counselor to be with you forever." But not only had God's companion Spirit been "with" the psalmist; he could not avoid or escape from God's presence (Ps. 139:7). There was no place to go where God was not there. Should the various possible places of escape be considered, such as the "heavens" or the "depths" (Hebrew *she'ol*, "grave"), as verse 8 suggests, they will prove to be futile. God is everywhere—in heaven and in Sheol! David, using strong poetic images, speaks of the "wings of the dawn" and the "far side of the sea" (v. 9). The first image is of the sunrise in the east, and the second refers to the west, for the Mediterranean Sea was always to the west, or "in back," of the Israelites. So even settling in the Far East or dwelling in the Far West could not put any real distance and separation between God and any of his mortals.

Surprisingly, David is taught that "even there" (v. 10), in extreme heights and extreme depths, in the distant east or distant west, God would extend his "right hand" to "guide" and "hold" him. Usually God's right hand is offered to keep us from stumbling or falling. The contrast between God's hand ("*your* hand" and "*your* right hand") and we who are mortals ("hold *me*") could not be more noticeable.

So if taking off to heaven, or lying in the grave, or journeying to the far corners of the globe do not aid our escape from God, what about hiding in the thick and oppressive "darkness" (vv. 11–12). Perhaps God's eye could not penetrate that cover. But that is not going to insulate me from God's notice either. The darkness is "as light to [God]" (v. 12c), and the "night will shine like the day."

There is an old mariner's chart, drawn up in 1525, which is now on display at the British Museum in London. It outlines the North American coastline with its adjacent waters. The cartographer made some unusual notations on areas in the map that represent regions that were not yet explored. For example, he wrote "Here be giants," and "Here be fiery scorpions," or "Here be dragons." Eventually the map came into the possession of Sir John Franklin, a British explorer in the early 1800s. Scratching out the fearful notations, he wrote instead these words across the map, "Here is God!"[5]

It is impossible to be cut off from the presence of God anywhere. Ask those who have tried to flee from him. Was Jonah successful in his hideout in the heart of the sea? Could Achan hide the forbidden souvenirs of war in his tent (Josh. 7) without divine knowledge? Could Ananias and Sapphira conceal the exact selling price of their property from God (Acts 5)? There is not one nook or cranny in the whole universe where God is not present.

III. Our God Is Omnipotent (Ps. 139:13–18)

To show the wonderful omnipotence of God, the psalmist chooses in this section to depict the marvelous development of a baby in his or her mother's womb. Within a tiny insignificant speck of liquid material, hardly visible to the naked eye, all the characteristics of the future child are contained: eyes, hair, skin, physical characteristics, and more. Some have totaled it up (in part) to contain sixty trillion cells, one hundred thousand miles of nerve fiber, sixty thousand miles of vessels carrying blood around the body, and some two hundred fifty bones, plus numerous joints, ligaments, and muscles. And some say this is not marvelous? It was God who "created [our] inmost being; [he] knit [us] together in [our] mother's womb" (v. 13). Who will dare say this creator is not omnipotent? God is the divine architect and engineer who put muscle, tissue, sinews, nerves, blood vessels, and bones together to make each of us.

It was God's eyes that saw our "unformed body," our "embryo" (Hebrew *golmi*), while you and I were still being put together in our mother's womb (vv. 14b–16). One might think that the embryo is something that is secret and beyond the sight and knowledge of anyone; but that is not so with God. In fact, "All the days ordained for me were written in [God's] book" (v. 16b). God's book is alluded to in Psalm 56:8; 69:28; and Exodus 32:32–33. One of God's books is the Lamb's Book of Life, in which all who believe in the Lord have their names inscribed. But this book in Psalm 139 seems to be a book in which the entirety of the psalmist's being and all his days and deeds are written down.

The effect that all this divine scrutiny and knowledge had on David was mind-boggling (v. 17). These thoughts about God's omniscience, omnipresence, and omnipotence are very "heavy" for David. The NIV calls them "precious," but they are both "valuable" and exceedingly "heavy" concepts to try to grasp. Indeed, "the sum of them" is "vast" and "great." In verse 18, when David proposes to "count" God's thoughts and deeds, he is not expressing the quantitative aspects of these thoughts, but rather that they are like the sand of the sea. It is a sheer impossibility to get any kind of assessment, much less an accurate count, of the number of grains of sand. In like manner, our God is so awesome in his character that he exceeds all boundaries and quantifiable categories we might attempt to place on him. He is magnificently great!

Conclusions

1. God cannot be compared or likened to anything or anyone we ever have known or ever could know.

2. God's omniscience, omnipresence, and omnipotence are so great that any puny mortal who dares turn against him is bound for real trouble. In fact, this psalm ends with verses 19–22 on the punishment of such rebels.

3. The character of God is the norm for who we are and what we would do and become. His character sets the norm and the standard for what is right, just, good, and ethical.

8

MAGNIFYING THE GLORY OF OUR GOD

EZEKIEL 1:1–28

Introduction

The concept of the "glory of the LORD" first appears in Exodus 16:7. God had promised to send manna after the people had bellyached and grumbled to Moses about how they missed the wonderful food they used to get in Egypt. Moses declared: "In the morning you will see the glory of the LORD" (Hebrew *kevod YHWH*). And in verse 10, as the congregation was looking toward the desert, "there was the glory of the LORD appearing in a cloud." This became a technical term for the Lord manifesting his presence to his people.[1] Thus, we judge that the glory of the Lord was something that could be "seen" and that it was connected with a "cloud."

"Glory" is uniquely a divine quality; in a very real sense only God has glory. His glory is exclusive, for he has said in Isaiah 42:8, "I will not give my glory to another or my praise to idols." To the extent that his glory is ever given to his creatures, it is a derivative kind of glory. King David understood that fact, for as he and the people collected the overwhelming number of gifts given to build the temple, he exclaimed in 1 Chronicles 29:11–12, "Yours, O LORD, is the greatness and the power and the glory and the majesty and the splendor, for everything in heaven and earth is yours." Surely "the heavens declare the glory of God" (Ps. 19:1), and "the whole earth is full of his glory" (Isa. 6:3), so that "all the peoples/nations see his glory" (Ps. 97:6).

The Hebrew word *kavod* denotes primarily what is heavy or weighty; then it comes to mean wealth, or a stance of honor that adds to a person's standing, position, or influence. When it is used of persons, it speaks of their prestige, honor, or reputation. But when used of God, it clearly marks out his power, his majesty, and his presence in all of his transcendent splendor, as in the phrase, "the glory of the Lord." Sometimes it is linked to a cloud (Exod. 24:15–18; 40:34–35; Num. 16:42 [17:7]; 1 Kings 8:11), but it would appear that it is always a cloud radiating light.

Glory, then, is a special term that depicts God's visible and active presence. In fact, "Yahweh's presence was so central and so significant in the Mosaic era that four terms [in addition to his *Shekinah* presence in the tabernacle day and night] are used to speak of it: the "face," "appearance," or "presence" of the Lord (*panim*); His glory (*kavod*); the "angel of the LORD" (*mal'ak YHWH*); and His "name" (*shem*)."[2] Thus, the glory of the Lord became closely associated with these terms, especially with the "name" of the Lord.

The best illustration of this can be seen in Moses's request, "Now show me your glory" (Exod. 33:18), on the occasion of Aaron's making the golden calf that caused all Israel to sin. Moses wanted assurance that God would not desert him or his people. Moses wanted to catch a whole new vision of who God was as an assurance that he and his people would not be left to their own deserts.

God's response was to "cause all [his] goodness to pass in front of [Moses], and . . . [to] proclaim [his] name, the LORD [Yahweh], in [Moses's] presence" (Exod. 33:19). Later, in verses 21–23, God told Moses, "There is a place near me where you may stand on a rock. When my glory passes by, I will put you in a cleft in the rock and cover you with my hand and you will see my back; but my face must not be seen."

In the one scriptural text, God causes his "goodness" to pass by, but in the other text, he causes his "glory" to pass by. Surely his goodness must be the sum total of all his being and essence. God, who is spirit, does not have a "hand," of course. Nevertheless, the meaning is clear. The radiance and effulgence of his glory will "pass by" "in front of" the cleft in the rock where God has protected Moses by his "hand" so that the full impact of the magnificence of the divine person does not blind him. However, Moses is allowed to see the "back," not the "face" of God. What is meant by God's back? For as a spiritual being, he does not have a back. If his glory and the glow of his magnificence is being demonstrated, and it has just passed by, then can we not render the idea of God's "back" as the "afterglow" of his glory that has just passed by?

The effect that this manifestation of the glory of God had on Moses is seen in Exodus 34:29–33. So intimidating is the radiance that is left on the face of Moses after being exposed merely to the "afterglow" of the radiance of God's presence, that Moses had to veil his face when he spoke with the people. Later, when he went into the presence of God again, he removed the veil until he came out to talk to the people to give them the word he had received from God.

G. L. Bray concluded,

> The interchangeableness or close association in this passage [Exod. 33–34] of God's glory and his presence/face, his goodness, his name and his radiance, both veiled and unveiled, and the fact that Moses both does, and yet may not see the Lord's face, indicates that God's glory is his manifest presence which, without further mediation, will destroy his creatures, but which admits of mediated expressions involving the most intimate fellowship with him. In the NT, Jesus Christ is the ultimate and permanent expression of divine glory (e.g., John 1:14; 2 Cor 3:13–14)."[3]

When the ark of the covenant, which also symbolized the presence of God, was taken from the Israelites in that infamous battle with the Philistines, it was appropriate that Eli's daughter-in-law name her son "Ichabod," meaning "no glory" (1 Sam. 4:21–22).

In addition to the concepts of presence, honor, and the manifestation of his magnificence, God's glory also speaks of his power. For example, the "appearance" (Hebrew mar'eh) of his glory in Exodus 24:17 was likened to a "consuming fire": "To the Israelites the glory of the LORD looked like a consuming fire on the top of the mountain." This also explains why Moses could not enter the tent of meeting in Exodus 40:34, for "the cloud covered the Tent of Meeting, and the glory of the LORD filled the tabernacle."

In the prophets of the Old Testament, God's glory takes on messianic proportions. The announcing voice declares that "the glory of the LORD will be revealed" to all humanity (Isa. 40:5). This glory is none other than our Lord Jesus himself.

But if the first advent is a place where God's glory is revealed in the person and presence of the Messiah, the Old Testament prophets are even more enthusiastic about a future messianically mediated appearance in the second advent, when Israel is also restored to her land (Isa. 35:2; 58:8; 59:19; 60:1–2, 13, 19; 62:2–3; 66:18, 19). Whereas God's glory has filled the tabernacle or the temple (Exod. 40:34–35; 1 Kings 8:11; 2 Chron. 7:1–2; Ezek. 10:4; Hag. 2:7) in the past, the writers of Scripture look forward to an even greater manifestation of God's glory that will one day fill the whole earth (Ps. 72:19; Hab. 2:14). From the east to the west, the nations will one day revere the glory of God universally. In order to help effect that grand day, God will send Israel's restored remnant to the nations that have not yet heard of God's fame or his glory, and they shall proclaim his glory among the nations (Isa. 66:19). Then the knowledge of the glory of the Lord will be as broad as the waters that cover the sea (Hab. 2:14).

Finally, the glory of God is a way that God refers to himself, especially when using suffixial forms, such as "my glory" (e.g., Isa. 66:19). It is little wonder, then, that the glory of the Lord is so prominent in the numerous doxologies in the New Testament (e.g., Rev. 1:6; 4:11; 5:12–13; 7:12; 19:1). God will display his glory and power in ways that are reminiscent of his work in the Old Testament. But most of all, it surely is a sign that he is actively and personally present.

An Exposition of Ezekiel 1:1–28

Surely Ezekiel is the prophet who majors on the theme of the glory of God. Ezekiel's book opens with a vision of the great throne of God on a chariot of unusual description. But despite the unusual imagery in this vision, in both chapter 1 and chapter 10, Ezekiel is quick to tell us what this vision was all about: "This was the appearance of the likeness of the glory of God" (Ezek. 1:28). Here, then, is the focal point of our passage and the source of our lesson or sermon title. Our interrogative will be "What?" and our homiletical key word will be "effects" produced by the glory of God.

    I. The Glory of Our God in the Windstorm and the Cloud (Ezek. 1:1–4)
   II. The Glory of Our God in the Living Creatures (Cherubim) (Ezek. 1:5–14)
  III. The Glory of Our God in the Wheels and the Throne-Chariot (Ezek. 1:15–21)
  IV. The Glory of Our God in the Platform and the Throne (Ezek. 1:22–27)

Ezekiel ministered from the land of his captivity, Babylon. When he was twenty-five years of age, in 597 BC, the Babylonian armies took the city of Jerusalem after a short resistance. Judah's king, Jehoiachin, had revolted against Babylonian rule, and so the Babylonians came to reestablish their sovereignty. Nebuchadnezzar skimmed off the top leadership of Judah, including Ezekiel. The prophet Jeremiah had predicted as much in Jeremiah 24, where he set forth the parable of the two baskets of figs. One was full of choice fruit, and the other was a basket of plain rotten fruit. It is not known whether it was a comfort to Ezekiel to know that he, as an exile, was included among the basket of choice fruit, but it surely must have grieved him to see his beloved country and city of Jerusalem once again in the grip of Babylonian rule. In five more years, on his thirtieth birthday, he could have been eligible for the priesthood (Num. 4:1, 3; 18:19, 39, 43) since his father, Buzi, was a priest of the order of Zadok. But instead of serving in the temple of God in Jerusalem, God had now appointed him to be a prophet in exile in the community of Tel Abib (Ezek. 3:15), near the River Kebar, which the Babylonians called the Grand Canal, a canal that flowed southeast of the Euphrates River at Babylon.

As the fortunes of Jerusalem were declining steadily, Babylon was booming. Ezekiel's soul must have been vexed to witness the magnificent hanging gardens, the massive fortifications, the startlingly beautiful architecture, the aggressive economy, and the ever-present evidences of idolatry on all sides with sexual excesses to the hilt. One day, as he looked northward and felt the hand of the Lord upon him (1:3), he saw an "immense cloud" (1:4) that was accompanied by flashes of lightning and enveloped in a light of burning brilliance. As Ezekiel proceeds to describe this vision, things seem to get weirder and weirder. In fact, it all is so strange that poor Ezekiel has been subjected to all sorts of psychological examinations by many unsympathetic commentators and preachers. He has been accused of being cataleptic, neurotic, hysterical, psychopathic, and evidencing definite signs of paranoid schizophrenia—as if these amateur pundits could resurrect him from the grave and put him on the psychiatrist's couch and examine him long distance with scientific accuracy! Obviously, this is all foisted on poor Ezekiel in accordance with current tastes and experiences. Instead, we will take the narrative on its own terms and let it say what it wishes, taking it at face value until we find convincing evidences to treat it otherwise.

What Ezekiel experienced was a "vision." A vision is normally not the same thing as a dream; it normally comes in a wide-awake experience, whereas dreams come normally in a state of sleep. Ezekiel claims to have experienced this same vision, or something like it, several times (Ezek. 1; 8:4; 10; 11:22–23; 43:3). The repetition of this experience allowed him to elaborate more on what he saw in each depiction of it.

Despondent as he must have been now in exile away from his beloved land of Israel, this prophet sensed that God "opened" the heavens (1:1) for him to see "visions of God." What an amazing antidote for depression and despondency: a whole new view of the majesty, mystery, and magnificence of God himself! Ezekiel's mind was opened to a degree he had not previously experienced, it would appear, for this vision of God came at a time when the exiles surely found themselves in hopeless depression. No one can see God and live, but neither can one live without seeing God in some form. If God does not reveal himself, how can mortals keep from being overwhelmed by the normal events of life itself, much less a captivity?

I. The Glory of Our God in the Windstorm and the Cloud (Ezek. 1:1–4)

The vision began with a whirling, mighty windstorm (v. 4) that built up into a powerful, towering cloud. Perhaps it was like a huge thunderhead or, even more terrifying in its appearance, like the funnel cloud of a tornado blowing into town. It was a foreboding and forbidding cloud that was surrounded by flashes of lightning and cracks of thunder. It glowed as if it were heated glass ready to be blown into different forms. That is why the center of the cloud was "like glowing metal" (v. 4).

Ezekiel was clear that this vision was the means God was using to bring "the word of the LORD" (v. 3) to him. God was allowing at least the effects of his presence to be seen in this towering, whirling, glowing, burning cloud. God himself was present in all his majesty and magnificence.

But there was more than a cloud; the cloud in verse 4 was followed by a description of "living creatures" (vv. 5–14) and then "wheels" (vv. 15–21). Then at the center and height of the whole vision was a platform/expanse and a throne (vv. 22–27). The mystery, obscurity, and marvel of this whole vision is a revelation of the being of God. The irresistibility, power, and awesomeness of God are presented to us in the closest images that our Lord can offer for those who need a whole new look at their magnificent Lord moving in power across the plains of time and history to complete his plan of salvation, even in the face of would-be conquerors and dominions.

II. The Glory of Our God in the Living Creatures (Cherubim) (Ezek. 1:5–14)

Out of the approaching storm, four living creatures emerged. This storm, with its mighty wind, came from the north (v. 4) and was accompanied by flashes of lightning (v. 13), but climaxed with a rainbow (v. 28). The theme of God manifesting himself in a storm is common to the ancient Near East and Scripture.

The four "living creatures" will appear later in Ezekiel 10 (vv. 5, 20) as "cherubim," angelic creatures who guard the holiness of God. Just as the cherubim were assigned to the Garden of Eden after the fall of Adam and Eve to prevent sinful humans from reentering the garden (Gen. 3:22–24), so here these living beings are tasked with preventing anything that is unholy from coming into the presence of God. The cherubim were selected to be embroidered on the curtain of the tabernacle, once again guarding the holy of holies and the holiness of God (Exod. 26:1). In the holy of holies, a representation of two cherubim stretched out over the ark of the covenant as they stood guard over the presence of God in all his holiness (Exod. 25:18–22). Thus, in this text in Ezekiel, the cherubim signaled the presence and the magnificence of God, even for the exiles in Babylon.

Many see ten characteristics of the living creatures/cherubim in verses 5–14.[4] Each of these characteristics appears to be related to some aspect of the work the cherubim were to perform. The ten characteristics are:

1. Each was "in appearance [in the] form . . . of a man" (v. 5). While each also had qualities and features that were nonhuman, starting with the human quality was a reminder of the fact that men and women are at the top of God's created order and the reason for his creation (Gen. 1:26–28; 2:8–25).
2. Each of the cherubim had four faces, one on each side (vv. 6, 10). One face represented the highest form in humanity (once again noting that humans were first as the crown of all creation), and there was one face for each category of the animal world: the lion for the wild kingdom, the ox for the domesticated kingdom, and the eagle for the bird kingdom.
3. The legs of the living creatures were straight (v. 7) without any joints, and at the foot they had hoofs like a calf. Briscoe suggests that this spoke of their "stability" for the assigned function of bearing the platform with the throne of God,[5] but that is uncertain since the wings of the creatures seemed to be free to flutter and fly.
4. "Under their wings on the four sides they had the hands of a man" (v. 8). Two wings of each creature stretched out to the next creature (v. 9), showing that they were united in performing their tasks.[6]

5. "Each one went straight ahead" (v. 9), for there was no need to turn in any direction since a face was on all four sides. Each direction taken was a movement forward in the functions assigned to them.

6. Each had two wings touching its neighbor and two wings covering its body (v. 11). Isaiah 6:2 and Revelation 4:1–11 describe similar creatures—Isaiah calls them "seraphim"—but those creatures had six wings each. Perhaps, as many suggest, the extra pair of wings was to hide their faces from gazing on the face of God, but in Ezekiel the creatures were under the platform and could not see the face of God. The two wings that covered their bodies may speak of their modesty and humility.

7. The living creatures went wherever the Spirit went (v. 12). Dan Block calls Ezekiel "the prophet of the Spirit,"[7] because Ezekiel refers to the Spirit fifty-two times. Block sees the use of the "spirit" here as the agency of animation, or as "the vitalizing principle of life that comes from God himself."[8]

8. The appearance of these creatures was like "burnished bronze," "burning coals of fire," and "torches" (vv. 7, 13). Whenever God appears in a theophany, it is usually accompanied with radiance, brightness, and brilliance because of his presence and nearness.

9. These creatures went so fast that their speed was "like flashes of lightning" (v. 14). The will of God was put into action almost simultaneously with the word from God, energized by the power of the Spirit.

10. The wings of these creatures made an enormous sound, "like the roar of rushing waters" (vv. 23–24). The prophet likened this amazing sound to the voice of God himself.

This sort of IMAX Technicolor presentation of how God works through his creatures in this world is enough to leave us with our mouths wide open and absolutely awestruck. These spiritual beings, who appeared part human, part angelic, and part animal, called the whole created order into demonstrating the awesomeness and the unrivaled glory of God. There was absolutely nothing like it in all the universe.

III. The Glory of Our God in the Wheels and the Throne-Chariot (Ezek. 1:15–21)

The chapter goes on, as do chapters 10 and 11 of Ezekiel, with a vision of the glory of God. Surely his glory goes way beyond anything mortals can put into human language, but still we can get at least an impression of what it is like. Ezekiel saw an extraordinary chariot that easily went in any direction needed without resistance or the need for a steering wheel. The wheels get a lot of attention in the text and were "like a wheel intersecting a wheel" (v. 16). This may indicate that these were caster-like wheels that easily swiveled in any direction the throne-chariot needed to go. The prophet thus had no need to fear that God would send him in a direction where the divine presence could not also go.

These wheels sat on the ground under the feet of the living creatures, who were under the platform on which was located the throne of God. When the cherubim moved, the wheels moved. But the strangest feature of the wheels was that their "rims were high and awesome, and all four rims were full of eyes" (v. 18). Apparently, the eyes symbolized the ability of God to see everything and all that went on in history (2 Chron. 16:9; Zech. 3:9; 4:10). Again, in addition to God's omnipotence, here was his omniscience. The fact that the wheels themselves were alive (v. 20) and full of eyes caused the Jewish *Targum* to list the wheels (Hebrew *'ofannim*) as another class of heavenly beings alongside seraphs, cherubs, and angels.

There was a close synchronization between the living creatures and the wheels, even though the wheels were not in any way attached to the living creatures. Nevertheless, wherever the wheels would go, there the living creatures would go and vice versa (v. 20). What motivated their synchronized movement was the "Spirit." Later, the "Spirit" would come into the prophet and raise him up and speak to him (Ezek. 2:2; 3:24). This would only be a foretaste of the role that the Holy Spirit would play in the life of the prophet and his book. It may well be that in verses 20 and 21, it was the "Spirit of life" (rather than the "spirit of the living creatures") that was in the wheels, meaning that the wheels somehow were animated in their movement by the Holy Spirit himself or by the vitalizing animation of the "spirit of life" that came from above.

IV. The Glory of Our God in the Platform and the Throne (Ezek. 1:22-27)

Attention now shifts from the wheels and the living creatures to what was above the living creatures, namely, a platform "sparkling like ice and awesome" (1:22). Under this "firmament," or "expanse," a pair of wings of each of the living creatures spread out tip to tip, while the other pair of wings of each creature covered its body. The wings do not seem to be holding up this platform, for the motion of the wings is described as "like the roar of rushing waters," "like the voice of the Almighty/*Shadday*" (an abbreviation for God's ancient name, El Shaddai), and "like the tumult of an army" (v. 24). Numerous literary parallels of this description can be found in Psalm 18:6-16.[9]

Quickly the center of all our attention is drawn toward the majestic throne that sat on the platform or expanse. The "voice" that came from the throne called the attention of everyone to this focal point of the whole scene. On this "throne of sapphire" "was a figure like that of a man/human being" (v. 26). But this was no ordinary human being, for "from . . . his waist up he looked like glowing metal, as if full of fire" (v. 27). The lower portion of his body was surrounded in a glow of fiery luminescence. Over the whole throne was what seemed like a rainbow, adding a more polychromatic, breathtaking aura and splendor to the magnificence of his person.

What are we to make of this almost indescribable depiction of the Lord God? Ezekiel is sure it was just a brief peek into the "glory of the LORD" (v. 28). Of all the theophanies in the Old Testament, none can match the multi-spectacular and polychromatic essence of Ezekiel's vision of God. This vision at once speaks of God's transcendence, his holiness as one who is absolutely distinct and different from all of creation, and that he is King enthroned over all. Yet he also is presented as one who is willing to condescend to a human form, to be made in the likeness of a man.[10]

The prophet Ezekiel, though now in Babylonian exile, was assured as he was called by God that no matter where he went, the living

God in all his magnificence and glory would go with him in any and every direction. Moreover, God would be with this prophet and with his people, no matter what land they were in. The theory of pagan theologies that tied each country's deity/deities to a specific piece of real estate so that god, people, and land all went together was incorrect. The presence of the Lord was most certainly and powerfully available to all who would live in faith and obedience. However, for the disobedient, thirteen months later this same heavenly chariot would return to transport the glory of God out of the temple and out of Jerusalem (Ezek. 9:3; 10:18–19; 11:22), not to return to the Holy City until that future day that the prophet mentioned years later in Ezekiel 43:1–5. So this chariot and vision of the glory of God could depict the impending judgment of God just as well as it so often depicted his abiding presence.

Conclusions

1. The majestic and powerful presence of the glory of God fired up the soul and mind of this called servant of God. With so awesome a God, how could he or we fail to sense the greatness of the God we serve?
2. The prophet Daniel witnessed a similar depiction of the fiery throne of God in Daniel 7, where the "Ancient of Days" was shown as seated on the throne until the "son of man" came "with the clouds of heaven" (Dan. 7:13).
3. Believers today need a glimpse of this same glorious Lord if worship is going to be what it should be, for how else will we ever be able to adequately give to God what he is "worth" in our "wor(th)ship"?

9

MAGNIFYING THE GRACE OF GIVING FROM OUR GOD

1 CHRONICLES 29:6–19

Introduction

Here in the tenth to the thirteenth verses of 1 Chronicles 29 is one of the greatest psalms David ever composed. For example, the magnificence of our Lord is described in just five carefully chosen words in verse 11 to give us a doxology to the high God of heaven who is infinite in time ("from everlasting to everlasting," v. 10), infinite in space ("everything in heaven and earth," v. 11), and infinite in authority ("You are exalted as head over all," v. 11). The five words that describe our Lord are:

His greatness,
His power,
His glory,
His majesty, and
His splendor.

So awesome were the sheer magnitude and the overwhelming nature of being confronted by such a wonderful Lord that "the people rejoiced at the willing response of their leaders, for they had given [their tithes and offerings] freely and wholeheartedly to the LORD" (1 Chron. 29:9).

There have been only a few times in history when God's people poured out so much so freely and with such joy that everyone was simply overwhelmed by what God had done in and through them to the honor and glory of his own name. But before we examine this text, it would be prudent for us to prepare our hearts, and those of our people, by examining in depth what lies behind one of the key themes raised by this passage: the theme of giving to the Lord.

In each of the preceding eight chapters we have focused on one main idea that helped us to get to the heart of one of the key issues in that text. Most often it was a theological concept, but in other cases it was the historical or archaeological background that helped to illumine the meaning of that text. In this chapter we are concentrating on the "grace of giving,"[1] for we want to learn what would have motivated these people to give so generously and so wholeheartedly that they would have to be told to stop their giving. At the root of it all, of course, was a special grace that God gives and that is still operative to this day. But it is precisely the lack of teaching on the joy of giving to our Lord that has tended to dampen our view of the magnificence of God, and left in its trail a vacuum of any blessing on the work of our hands or that of our church and other institutions. That raises the question, then: what does Scripture teach about this grace of giving that comes from God?

Long before the law of Moses urged the people to bring a tenth of all their earnings to the Lord (a principle known as "tithing"), the patriarch Abraham practiced exactly the same thing as he gave tithes to God (Gen. 14:17–20). This was, we must remember, some six hundred years before the law was given, so it is not possible to charge that such a practice is legalistic and out of bounds for the church in this, or any other, age of grace. Moreover, Abraham gave these gifts to a priest-king of "Salem" (probably an old name for "Jerusalem" before it was captured, approximately a thousand years later, by the Israelites) named Melchizedek. Melchizedek is otherwise unknown to us, except that he too professed belief in Yahweh and thanked God for Abraham's great victory and his rescue of Abraham's nephew, Lot. Abraham gave to Melchizedek a tithe of all the spoils that he had captured in the battle against the four kings who had come up from Mesopotamia against the five cities of the plain (on the east side of the Dead Sea in what is today the modern state of Jordan). Later, in Hebrews 7, Melchizedek will be presented as a type of our Lord Jesus.

Thus, just as Melchizedek gave Abraham bread and wine, and Abraham showed his indebtedness to God by freely rendering to Melchizedek tithes from his spoils, so our Lord serves us the symbols of his service for our redemption in the bread and the wine, and we in turn, out of gratitude, acknowledge our indebtedness to him by our tithes and offerings.

In addition to our tithes, we also can give God our "offerings." These offerings represent our "freewill giving," which is over and above our usual tithes of ten percent. Therefore, at a minimum, we must give God our tithes, for he ordered us to do so. But God *deserves* our offerings, which represent our voluntary gifts and demonstrate the overflow of our hearts in the joy and gratitude we have for so great a Savior and so great a salvation.

Tithing, then, appeared almost six hundred years before the law was given. It was codified in the law of God (Lev. 27:30–33), it was also approved by our Lord (Matt. 23:23), and it was continued in the teaching and instruction given by the apostle Paul (1 Cor. 16:2). This can hardly be a matter of passing curiosity; it is both ancient and contemporary in its significance.

It is God's word, then, that teaches us to set aside the first part of our income for the Lord (Deut. 14:22–23; Prov. 3:9–10). Our giving must not be out of what is left over after we pay for everything we want to do with our funds; it must represent the first part of our income. Not only should we give our tithe, or tenth, of our income to the Lord, but our desire also should be to give voluntary "offerings" over and above that tithe just to show how grateful we are to the Lord.

The great Old Testament teaching passage on tithing is Malachi 3:7–15. It begins where all great giving to the Lord must begin—with repentance and a full turning back to the Lord: " 'Return to me, and I will return to you,' says the LORD Almighty" (Mal. 3:7). Yet, when this challenge was first given by the prophet Malachi, the people protested: "How are we to return?" (v. 7b). Their hollow protest indicated that they felt comfortable with themselves and their relationship to the Lord. Where was the problem?

God had the prophet put his finger on one of the most obvious examples of how Malachi's audience was wandering from God. He charged them with robbing God (v. 8). Again, the people protested, "How do we rob [God]?" (v. 8). Malachi boldly answered: "In tithes and offerings" (v. 9). The whole nation was under a "curse" because they had failed to "bring the whole tithe into the storehouse, that there may be food in my [God's] house" (v. 10).

Many find such teaching to be very hard, but the principle of material giving to God is bound up with the idea of God blessing nations, churches, or individuals or withholding his favor from them. Accordingly, any and all forms of withholding our tithes and offerings from God only invites God to get our attention by withholding his blessing from the work of our hands as well. It is not that God is vindictive or peevish about our lack of giving, but rather that he wants us to enjoy all the joy and blessings he has for us. If we become tone-deaf and resistant to the teaching of his word, he will still speak to us through the events of our lives, just because he still loves us.

Amazingly, God invited the people of Malachi's day (as he does us) to "test [him] . . . and see if [he] will not throw open the floodgates of heaven and pour out so much blessing that [we] will not have room enough for it" (v. 10b). Look how lavish this challenge is. The "windows of heaven" will be opened to pour down on us God's blessing? Really? The figure of speech here is even more graphic in the Hebrew text. God says he will continue to pour out such blessing "until there is no more [room to contain it. Or is it that he will pour out so much it runs the risk of bankrupting heaven?]." Obviously this is hyperbole, for how could God in his heaven, as it were, run dry of reciprocal gifts to match our generosity? Or, alternatively, could we exhaust the means and capacity to receive it all? Could we mortals actually outgive God and put such a run on the bank of heaven that God would have to temporarily close down his offer?

What a challenge! The high and exalted Lord of all creation invites mortals such as we are to "test" and "prove" him! Amazing! The end of such generous giving is that "all the nations will call [us] blessed, for [ours] will be a delightful land" (v. 12). Not only will the surrounding nations of the earth see the prosperity God has poured out on that nation that really obeys him and has taken him up on his challenge, but these same nations also will give thanks to God for the gospel that has come to them through the generosity of God's people.

This is not to say that such giving is not costly. David recognized this principle when Araunah the Jebusite offered his threshing floor to David as a site for an altar to the Lord; he also offered oxen and wood for the sacrifices at no cost to David. King David insisted on paying Araunah for the site and the animals, saying, "I will not sacrifice to the LORD my God burnt offerings that cost me nothing" (2 Sam. 24:24). So we too can give only what actually costs us; otherwise it has no value and comes with no sense of priority or respect for God's person.

To this study of Old Testament texts we can add the New Testament teaching on the laws of harvest that operate not only in the natural realm but in the spiritual realm as well. Second Corinthians 9:6–9 announces that the one who sows in a stingy way will reap very "sparingly." But those who sow "generously" in both the natural and spiritual realms will realize very generous returns. So the apostle Paul urges us to give, but to do so from the heart, "not reluctantly or under compulsion, for God loves a cheerful giver. And God is able to make *all* grace abound to [*all* who do so], so that in *all* things at *all* times, having *all* that you need, you will abound in *every* good work" (2 Cor. 9:7–8, emphasis mine). It is almost as if Paul could not think of another "all" to put in this text, for he was most excited to show us how the law of the harvest works. Such giving is an investment, for sowing is more than mere scattering. It must be done orderly and purposefully, but always with great joy and cheerfulness. It is, after all, a gift to the high and holy Lord of all creation who has given us the grace to give in the first place.

Lest some think that this teaching is only a ruse to get a raise for the teacher/preacher, or a plot to milk God's people out of their hard-earned money, note that Jesus himself in his parables taught more often on money than on any other topic. Bruce Waltke has noted that politicians say, "It's the economy stupid," but it is not even about the economy, my possessions, or even about me; it is all about thee.[2] If we fail to teach on this topic, we fail to follow our Lord's example and his emphasis as well.

With this as a backdrop, let us now turn to our passage on the awesomeness of God in 1 Chronicles 29:6–19.

An Exposition of 1 Chronicles 29:6–19

The subject comes from the focal point, or the big idea, found in verse 11: "Yours, O LORD, is the greatness and the power and the glory and the majesty and the splendor." The reason for this jubilant outbreak of praise to God was the beautiful expression of whole-hearted and willing giving of the leaders and the people of God as they prepared to build the temple of God.

How (our interrogative), then, was this awesomeness of God to be manifested in this call to give their tithes and offerings for the raising of the temple of God? It was seen in at least three ways (our homiletical word):

    I. In the Magnificence of God's Person (1 Chron. 29:10–13)
   II. In the Magnificence of God's Grace (1 Chron. 29:14–15)
  III. In the Magnificence of God's Motivation for Us to Give (1 Chron. 29:6–9; 16–19)

I. In the Magnificence of God's Person (1 Chron. 29:10–13)

King David led the way and set the pattern for the giving habits of all the leaders and people. He pledged: "With all my resources I have provided for the temple of my God" (1 Chron. 29:2). It was on that basis that he then offered this challenge: "Now, who is willing to consecrate himself today to the LORD?" (v. 5).

How different was David's attitude from that of John Jacob Astor, who, though exceedingly rich, said, "I am the most miserable man on earth." John D. Rockfeller agreed: "I have made many millions, but they have brought me no happiness." Likewise, Henry Ford testified, "I was happier when [I was] doing a mechanic's job." Even W. H. Vanderbilt, of the fabulous Biltmore Estate and other magnificent properties, concluded, "The care of $200 million [quite a sum in those days] is enough to kill anyone. There is no pleasure in it."

Not so with King David, for David found that his chief delight was in giving his gifts to the Lord and in praising the God of gods and Lord of lords. He gave "three thousand talents of gold" (v. 4), which amounted to 110 tons (or 100 metric tons) of gold! If gold today is roughly worth $600 per ounce, then that gift alone was worth $2.112 billion. David also gave seven thousand talents of silver, which comes to approximately 260 tons (or 240 metric tons). If silver sometimes runs as high as $13 per ounce in today's markets, then that gift was worth in current dollars somewhere near $108.2 million. But add to that the gifts from the leaders and the people (vv. 7–8), and you have another $3.648 billion in gold and $117 million in silver, not to mention the gifts of "precious stones" (v. 8). This was an enormous outpouring of love and sacrifice to our most awesome Lord.

After such an offering of almost $6 billion in gold and almost $228 million in silver,[3] you would think it would be time to praise the king and all the people for such a generous offering they had made to God. But that is not how they felt about this matter; instead, David led the people in praising the Lord (v. 10). The Lord, who is infinite in *time* ("from everlasting to everlasting," v. 10d), and infinite in *space* ("everything in heaven and earth is yours," v. 11c), and infinite in *authority* ("You are exalted as head over all," v. 11d), had no rival that could come even close to the sheer awesomeness of his person. They magnified the living God as King of kings and Lord of lords, without comparison or a rival anywhere!

There were five areas in our Lord's uniqueness that were singled out for special mention in verses 10–13. First was his "greatness."[4] Primarily, God's "greatness" refers to his "mighty acts" (Ps. 145:3, 6). Often the words "mighty acts" were just another way to point to God's miraculous works on behalf of Israel and all he has redeemed. Another of God's "mighty acts" was giving his covenantal promise to David in 2 Samuel 7:21. God performed this "greatness" "for the

sake of [his] word and according to [his] will," which David here
calls a "great thing," namely, the promise to give David a dynasty,
kingdom, and throne forever (2 Sam. 7:16). This action is nothing
less than the very centerpiece of God's works, the promise-plan
given to Abraham that he would become a great nation (Deut. 4:6,
7, 8; 26:5). Even more revealing was the divine action in "driving
out nations and their gods from before [his] people" (2 Sam 7:23).
The magnitude of God's works is so stupendous that mortals cannot
comprehend them (Job 37:5; cf. Job 5:9; 9:10). Even the very "name"
of God is great (Josh. 7:9; 1 Sam. 12:22; 1 Kings 8:42; 2 Chron. 6:32;
Ps. 76:1; 99:3; Jer. 10:6; 44:26; Ezek. 36:23; Mal. 1:11).

The second unique quality of God is his "power."[5] Ultimately, all
strength and power belong to God. It is no surprise then to note
that in the rabbinic age, when it was forbidden to utter the name of
Yahweh, the Hebrew word for "power/strength" was used instead
as a substitute for God's name. It would appear that Jesus himself
illustrated that same usage when at his trial before Caiaphas he said
in Matthew 26:64 that he would be seen sitting at the right hand of
"Power" (NASB) and coming with the clouds of heaven. Clearly
he was identifying himself with God, which to the Jews of that day
was an obvious instance of "blasphemy." Note that God's power is
usually associated with the spirit of wisdom and understanding,
of counsel and knowledge (Isa. 11:2; Job 12:13; Prov. 8:14). But all
power belongs uniquely to our Lord.

His also is the "glory." Rather than using the usual Hebrew word
for "glory" (kavod), David uses tif'ereth,[6] meaning "glory, dignity,
fame." However, in this passage God's glory—both his inherent and
ascribed glory—is seen as the effect created by the sheer magnificence
of the divine presence. That presence expresses the dignity of the one
bearing it as well as it elicits ascriptions of praise for all that that glory
has done. In Psalm 96:6, "splendor and majesty" are before the Lord
while "strength and glory" are in his sanctuary. God's presence/glory
(kavod) fills the whole earth (Isa. 6:3). Accordingly, this word shows
the dignity and beauty of our Lord's position as well as the fact that
he is personally present everywhere, showing the "power/arm of his
glory" (Isa. 63:12), leading his people so as to demonstrate a "name
of glory" (Isa. 63:14; 1 Chron. 29:13), and claiming that heaven itself

is the habitation of his glory (Isa. 60:7). God's fame and dignity far outclass all rivals in these same categories.

The fourth quality for which God is praised is his "majesty" (Hebrew *hod*).[7] Kings, of course, are ascribed a certain type of majesty, but kings also should be the first to honor God as the only true source of all royal honor and majesty. The majesty of God's voice is heard by the Assyrians in Isaiah 30:30, terrifying them. But in Habakkuk 3:3 a theophany covers the sky with God's majesty. God has set his majesty above the sky in Psalm 8:1.

God is ascribed praise not only for his greatness, power, glory, and majesty, but also for his "splendor" (Hebrew *netsah*).[8] In 1 Samuel 15:29, the Lord is called "The Splendor/Glory of Israel." Whereas the Greek Septuagint version rendered this word in 1 Chronicles 29:11 as *nike*, "victory," it is just as easy to see a greater connection with the idea of "perpetuity" and "lastingness," as the Hebrew parallelism of Psalm 13:1 and 16:11 would illustrate.

How awesome is the person of our Lord! David, on behalf of the whole gathered congregation, exalted the Lord by saying, "Now, our God, we give you thanks, and praise your glorious name" (1 Chron. 29:13). Anything less would have been an insult to the living God and ignorance on the part of all worshipers. Truly, our God is an awesome God!

The kingdom, rule, and reign belong exclusively to our God. Nothing is outside the sphere of his management. It is in his hands to disburse everything, for he gives strength and health to all. He also gives power, and it is he alone who exalts and raises persons up to positions of authority and responsibility. God apportions everything: all possessions, all music, all marriages, all wealth, all wisdom, all authority, and all culture. No wonder we are called to look to him alone. There is not one speck of the universe, possessions, or persons that God does not lay claim to as their creator and preserver and say, "Mine!"

II. In the Magnificence of God's Grace (1 Chron. 29:14-15)

Because of God's magnificence, we are all asked two questions: "Who are [we]?" (v. 14a) and how is it "that we should [have been] able to give as generously as this?" (v. 14b).

The point is that in comparison with so great a Lord, we are far outside of God's class and being. We are unfit and unworthy even to offer anything to so majestic a heavenly Father. These rhetorical questions remind us of how David responded to the Lord when he was told that the promise-plan of God was going to be given to him and to his family. He retorted, "Who am I, O LORD God, and what is my family, that you have brought me this far?" (1 Chron. 17:16). Yes, who are we indeed? Nothing and no one compares to our God!

The reason for our feeling so small in the presence of God is not only because of his person, but also because "everything comes from [God himself]" (v. 14c). There is nothing that we own of which we can say, "That's mine. I earned it." No, it came as a gift from God. Moreover, what we give back to God is "what comes from [God's] hand" (v. 14d). That is where God's grace comes in. It is he who has been gifting us as evidence of his grace and favor.

Never mind all the possessions we have accumulated, for our real home is not here, but in heaven. On this earth "we are aliens and strangers in [God's] sight" (v. 15a). Our days pass "like a shadow" (v. 15b), as "a mist" (James 4:14), or "as flowers of the field" (1 Pet. 1:24), or "as a mere handbreadth" (Ps. 39:5).

So in comparison with how little time we have here, all our material prosperity means little if it, like everything else that God gives, is not used and invested for the advancement of his awesome name and glory.

III. In the Magnificence of God's Motivation for Us to Give (1 Chron. 29:6-9, 16-19)

What made these gifts so memorable and spectacular? These gifts were great because the king, leaders, and people first gave themselves to the Lord before they gave their gifts (cf. 2 Cor. 8:5). Three times the text stresses that they all gave "willingly" (vv. 6, 9, 17). There was no need to ask, as Moses had to do in the golden calf incident, "Who is on the Lord's side?" (Exod. 32:26 KJV). The motivations of all, from top to bottom, had been stirred by the grace of God. True, the king set the pace (vv. 2–5), the leaders gave next (v. 8), and the people gave next (v. 9), but the motivations of all of them were crystal clear. It was a "wholehearted" giving, and it was giving not to mortals but to the Lord (v. 9d).

God did test their hearts, and David notes that what pleases God is "integrity" (v. 17a). But it was all done "willingly and with honest intent" (v. 17b).

David's prayer, as ours should be, was this: "Keep this desire in the hearts of your people forever" (v. 18). Once again, note how the moral state of the heart had to correspond to the nature of the gifts brought (cf. Mal. 1:10). This is what real living and real giving are all about: our chief goal in life ought to be to please God and to enjoy him forever. Imagine the sheer privilege—not to mention the enormous delight!—to bring back to God what God has given to us in the first place. That was what David, his leaders, and people experienced as they brought the funds to pay for the materials for the house of God that King Solomon was later to build.

Conclusions

1. All too frequently our hearts cling to our wealth, possessions, and talents for security and personal significance when our hearts first should have been given over to God and then indulged in the grace and joy of giving to so great and so awesome a God.
2. The question must be asked: is there a proportional relationship between how great God is in our eyes and how willing and how generous our gifts to this great God are?
3. Does our responsiveness in giving indicate something about the state of our hearts before God?

10

MAGNIFYING THE HOLINESS
OF OUR GOD

ISAIAH 6:1–13

Introduction

The English word *holy* is derived from the Anglo-Saxon *halig*, or *hal*, meaning "well," or "whole." The Hebrew word for "holy" is *qodesh*, which means "withheld from the ordinary use," "treated with special care," and "belonging to the sanctuary."[1] Even though there are holy people, holy places, holy garments, holy ointment, and holy food, the point is that these are holy not in and of themselves but because they all belong to God. This brings us back to what the word basically means: set apart from ordinary or common use and dedicated to God's use. Thus things and people do not become holy by some sort of magic but by being set apart and dedicated to God.

Therefore, when God is present, the ground becomes "holy ground" (Exod. 3:5). When God indwells the inner sanctum of the tabernacle, it becomes the "holy of holies." Even the people of God were a "holy people," not by moral accomplishments of their own, but simply because God had chosen them and set them apart for himself (Exod. 19:5; Lev. 20:26). They were holy in status, but rarely if ever in character and life.

It is for this reason that the moral demand was (and continues to be) placed on the people of God: "Be holy because I, the LORD your God, am holy" (Lev. 19:2, and frequently thereafter). Clearly, holiness signals a line of separation and a mark of ownership. Here is the great divide between God and mortals, between God and the world. Hosea 11:9 spells it out: "I am God, and not man—the Holy One among you."

While the word *transcendent* is not a biblical word, the nearest equivalent for the concept of transcendence is "holy."[2] As such, it is one of the most significant words in the Old Testament. So much does it sum up the whole nature of God that it can stand alone as his name in Isaiah 40:25—"'To whom will you compare me? Or who is my equal?' says the Holy One." God is frequently designated in the Old Testament as "the Holy One" (Job 6:10; Isa. 43:15; Ezek. 39:7; Hos. 11:9; Hab. 1:12; 3:3) or as "the Holy One of Israel" (2 Kings 19:22; Isa. 1:4; 43:3; Jer. 50:29; 51:5). In Isaiah 57:15, God is described as "the high and lofty One . . . who lives forever, whose name is holy."

One particular psalm, Psalm 99, is especially devoted to the holiness of God in that it seems to be an echo of the *trisagion* of the seraphim in Isaiah 6, who also respond in praise, "Holy, holy, holy." Psalm 99 uses the phrase "he is holy" three times, in verses 3, 5, and 9, to distinguish and mark out the strophes and to set the framework for the psalm. It depicts Yahweh seated on his throne over the living beings, or cherubim, as in Ezekiel 1 and 10. The verbs in verses 1 and 3 are best rendered as future tenses: "the nations shall be troubled, . . . the earth shall be moved, . . . [and the nations] shall praise [God's] great and awesome name." The nations and peoples of the earth are invited to "worship at his footstool" (v. 5), which in 1 Chronicles 28:2 is identified with the ark of God. This emphasis on "he is holy" shows that God's innermost being is altogether separate from what we mortals are, for he is pure and distinct from all things in this world and from all mortals, for his thoughts, purposes, and works are without any sin or fault.

A. W. Tozer, in his classic book *The Knowledge of the Holy*, writes,

> Until we have seen ourselves as God see [sic] us, we are not likely
> to be much disturbed over conditions around us as long as they do
> not get out of hand as to threaten our comfortable way of life. We
> have learned to live with unholiness and have come to look upon it
> as the natural and expected thing. We are not disappointed that we
> do not find all truth in our teachers or faithfulness in our politicians
> or complete honesty in our merchants or full trustworthiness in our
> friends. . . . Quite literally a new channel must be cut through the
> desert of our minds to allow the sweet water of truth that will heal
> our great sickness to flow in. We cannot grasp the true meaning of
> divine holiness by thinking of someone or something very pure and
> then raising the concept to the highest degree we are capable of. God's
> holiness is not simply the best we know infinitely bettered. We know
> nothing like divine holiness. It stands apart, unique, unapproachable,
> incomprehensible and unattainable.[3]

The concept of holiness has exercised a major influence in recent
generations of scholars, mainly, it would seem, through the influence of the book *The Idea of the Holy* by the Protestant theologian
Rudolph Otto (1869–1937).[4] Otto argued that there is in the human
mind something he called the "numinous," which he defined as a
vague, incomprehensible, and indefinable *mysterium tremendum*, a
mystery that envelopes and surrounds the whole universe. Unfortunately, this numinous or *mysterium tremendum* is always an "It," an
awe-full thing that can never be intellectually described; it is only
felt and experienced in the depths of the human spirit.

Otto did not agree with the liberal theologians of his day that
religion could be reduced to ethics. Rather, he felt that mortals do
have a religious nature that can and does respond to the awesome and
the mysterious in their very beings, a reality that can be summarized
in the word *holy*, or the experience of the "numinous."

Otto's concept of holiness, however, was anchored not in the
character of God, but in an affective experience. Strangely enough,
he made no reference to Leviticus 19, one of the key chapters on
holiness in the Bible. And in his deep desire to show that the holy
is a unique character of religion, Otto ended up making the ethical

aspect of holiness a mere "extra." He was correct, however, in sensing
that the feeling of mystery, even the majesty of our God, is so basic
to human nature that it cannot be avoided. But that in itself is not
enough. Instead of sensing that there is some "Thing filled with Awe"
out there, Otto needed to learn that this awe-full presence is not a
thing but a person, a moral being with all the qualities of warmth and
personality. Sure, there is a sense of wonder and fear in the presence
of so great a mystery, but it is also possible to say, "He is the Holy
One." Herein lies the great difference between the concepts of the
gods of ancient religions and the revelation of Holy Scripture:

> The character of God stands behind the moral duties for humanity.
> Other ancient religions did not appeal to the person, nature or actions
> of their deities as the basis for moral thinking and acting (cf. Psalm
> 82). Often the pagan deities were more sensual and debased in their
> actions and character than the mortals who strove to worship them.
> Not so with Yahweh, who is holiness itself and a model for all.[5]

Furthermore, "God's name," noted J. Alec Motyer, "is qualified
by the adjective 'holy' in the Old Testament more often than by all
other qualifiers put together."[6] Given the fact that holiness in its
etymology suggests both "separateness" and "brightness," this raises
the further question as to what makes our God so separate and so
brilliant in his distinctiveness. The answer that Motyer gave is that
it is God's "total and unique moral majesty. . . . When people fear
before God, it is not consciousness of . . . humanity in the presence
of divine power, but the consciousness of . . . sin in the presence of
moral purity."[7] Thus holiness manifests what is reserved and held
back of the glory of God, while his glory is the manifestation of his
majestic presence. It is in this light, then, that it is appropriate that
we look at Isaiah 6, the greatest biblical announcement and description of the holiness of God.

An Exposition of Isaiah 6:1–13

Isaiah was the prophet who saw God in all his majesty, holiness,
and glory. God, who is supremely known as "the Holy One of Is-

rael," is presented in Isaiah's prophecy under this title some twenty-nine times, while it is used only seven times in the rest of the Old Testament. It is little wonder then that in this chapter emphasis is placed on the threefold repetition of "Holy, holy, holy is the LORD Almighty" (Isa. 6:3). This text, then, will serve as the focal point, or big idea, of this chapter.

The best literary analysis of this chapter that I have seen is given by Motyer, who noted that the whole chapter is built around the three times that the prophet responds, "And I said" (Isa. 6:5, 8, 11; Hebrew wa'omar).[8] Based on Motyer's idea and general outline, I would suggest the following structure for teaching or preaching this passage. How, we ask in our interrogative, may we magnify the holiness of our God? There are three "ways" (to use our homiletical key word once again) that we may do so. They are:

I. By Our Responding to God's Holiness (Isa. 6:1-7)
   A. The Crisis Faced in the Death of a Competent King
   B. The Hope Gathered from a Theophany of the Heavenly Temple
   C. The Centrality of the Seraphim's Trisagion Song
   D. The Messenger's Awareness of His Own Uncleanness
   E. The Grace of God in Cleansing His Messenger
II. By Our Responding to God's Call (Isa. 6:8-10)
   A. God Issues His Call
   B. God Hears the Response to His Summons
   C. God Announces His Message to His Messenger
   D. God Describes the Task of His Messenger
III. By Our Responding to God's Purpose (Isa. 6:11-13)
   A. There Will Be a Time Limit
   B. There Will Be Desolation and Desertion of the Land and Cities
   C. There Will Be a Seed of Holiness Out of the Stump

I. By Our Responding to God's Holiness (Isa. 6:1-7)

A. *The Crisis Faced in the Death of a Competent King.* Chapter 6 functions both as the climax to Isaiah 1-5 and the prologue to chapters 7-12. Naturally, the death of King Uzziah around 740 BC[9] made Isaiah aware of the tendentious nature of the political situation as things entered a transitional stage. Isaiah had announced "woe" on the nation for one sin after another in the opening five chapters of his book (e.g., Isa. 5:8, 11, 18, 20, 21). But in this scene of the majestic holiness of God, he suddenly realized, "Woe [is] me!" (v. 5), as well. This would seem to indicate that while the call of God for service came from God himself, it was reinforced by the events of the day and the strong need on the part of his people and the nation for reconciliation with a holy God.

So the long and prosperous reign of King Uzziah came to an end (2 Kings 15:1–7; 2 Chron. 26) just as the nation was entering troubled times internationally and spiritually. Out of the Assyrian Empire arose the triumphant, imperialistic King Tiglath-pileser III, who began his reign in 745 BC. What would the nation do now that it had lost King Uzziah, its best defender of godly life and rule (until his pride later in his life led to his downfall), especially given the moral and doctrinal drift of the nation—not to mention that of the good king himself? It is most unusual in the biblical record to date events by the death of a king. Isaiah also does this in 14:28, where he sees similar significance in the death of King Ahaz. But why does he do this instead of using a more common notation such as, "In the fifty-second year of Uzziah, I saw the LORD"? Isaiah is an observer of history and of his own times. Accordingly, Uzziah's death served as another symbol to Isaiah of the nation's alienation and separation from God, which exposed it to God's displeasure. As surely as the darkness of death closed in around King Uzziah, so it likewise closed in around the nation.

B. *The Hope Gathered from a Theophany of the Heavenly Temple.* Against the dreary background that seemed to defy all hope, Isaiah suddenly "saw the Lord" (v. 1). Of course, John 1:18 clearly teaches that "No one has ever seen God," for God is incorporeal and is spirit (Isa. 31:3; John 4:24). However, God has condescended from time to time to allow one or another *aspect* of his person to be visible in some form or manner (e.g., as "commander of the Lord's army," Josh. 5:13–15).

Nevertheless, what was visible to God's servant is not so much a picture of God himself as it was an image of heaven, filled with background settings—robes, a throne, and attendants. God's presence and sovereignty are most real, but he himself is not described. God is pictured as seated on a throne, "high and exalted" (v. 1), which Motyer noted was the same pair of words used of the Servant of the Lord in Isaiah 57:15 (translated in the NIV as "high and lofty One").[10]

Not only was God seen seated on his throne, but also the place where his throne was located was the "temple" (v. 1), a word (*hekhal*) that most note is loaned to Hebrew from the Sumerian language of the third millennium BC as E.GAL, meaning "big house." Originally it referred to either the house of the god or the house of the king. In this case, the prophet was taken in vision form right into the heavenly temple, the palace of God. The contrast of the palace of Uzziah, now crestfallen by his death, with the joy of the abiding palace-temple of the eternal and sovereign God could not be more striking. It is this vision of the magnificence of God that will be more than enough to fix the sights and ministry of God's servant. There is no other place or preparation that can rival what the worship of the living God himself can provide for all who venture forth to serve him.

C. *The Centrality of the Seraphim's Trisagion Song.* These heavenly beings, called seraphs, or "burning ones," are found only in this passage. Ezekiel called those who accompanied the throne of God in Ezekiel 1 and 10 "living beings" or "cherubim." They had two pairs of wings, whereas these seraphim have three pairs: "With two wings they covered their faces, with two they covered their feet, and with two they were flying," observed Isaiah in verse 2. All three verbs indicate continuous action in the Hebrew text (cf. Ezek. 1:14). Since Ezekiel's "living beings" were under the pavement that supported the throne, apparently there was no necessity for two additional wings to cover their faces since they apparently could not see what was above them, but here in Isaiah it was necessary to prevent the seraphim from prying into the mystery and awesomeness of the immortal God.

But the most important feature of these seraphim was not their wings, their feet, or their flying; instead it was their calling out (to each other, perhaps antiphonally?) their song of exuberance: "Holy, holy, holy is the LORD Almighty; the whole earth is full of his glory" (v. 3). Hebrew uses repetition to show emphasis, thus the threefold repetition makes clear that what is most outstanding about our God who is now calling Isaiah to his service is God's holiness. Instead of merely communicating in verbal forms the transcendent aspects of his person, God called the emotive, the numinous, the imaginative, and the nonrational aspects of the prophet's being into play. This was done in order to suggest something more of the grandeur and magnificence of his being. Isaiah is to catch a glimpse of the distinctiveness and separateness of God. The same word "holy" (Hebrew *qodesh*) brought the sacred and the secular into mortal conflict, as can be shown from the fact that women who prostituted themselves to Baal and Asherah in sexual orgies were literally called "holy ones" (Hebrew *qedeshoth*, translated in the NIV as "shrine prostitutes," or "harlots"; cf. Gen. 38:21; Hos. 4:14). Both were "set apart," "separated unto" another being; in one case they were set apart to the Lord, but in the other they were "separated unto" harlotry. This is why we say that God is different and separate from all we know and experience. "Unique, unique, unique," would capture a good part of the song these seraphim sang continuously as worship continued in the heavenly precincts.

It is not clear why the "thresholds shook" or why "the temple was filled with smoke" (v. 4b). Perhaps it fits our contemporary expression that says, "the place rocked!" Anyway, that is how the earth generally reacts to the presence of God (cf. Exod. 19:18; Hab. 3:3–10). So thunderous was the acclamation that it seemed as if the very foundations of the temple of God would give way. In like manner, the smoke may be understood as the smoke of the incense, reminding us of the prayers of the saints that were being offered up to God the Father in the book of Revelation, or reminiscent of the cloud that signified the presence and glory of God in the tabernacle and the temple. In any case, all of this simply added to the effect as sight, sound, smell, and the prophet's entire sensory faculties were raised to their peak level in this meeting with the holy King of glory.

D. *The Messenger's Awareness of His Own Uncleanness.* At first the prophet of God was so overawed that his own unworthiness flooded into his consciousness. Instead of pronouncing woes on his people and nation, he suddenly pronounced a woe on himself.

He thought himself "ruined," or more accurately, according to one rendering of the Hebrew text, "silenced," that is, forbidden to join in the heavenly song. His own sin now presented itself to him in stark contrast to the presence of the crystal-clear purity and holiness of his Lord and Master. What could a finite, mortal, fallible sinner say or do in the presence of one who was so separate and so strikingly opposite to himself? "Immortal, invisible, God only wise, in light, inaccessible hid from our eyes," the prophet could just as well have sung. What a startling contrast to the mortal King Uzziah, who had just passed away! But life does not depend upon mortal kings, but upon the King of kings, who alone is holy and glorious. Isaiah had seen the King in all his fullness—yes, in all his holiness and different-ness.

E. *The Grace of God in Cleansing His Messenger.* Without any request for cleansing from God's servant, or even any promissory vows from the prophet if only God would cleanse him, God himself took the initiative to cleanse his servant. A "live coal" (v. 6) was brought from the altar of the heavenly temple. This altar was the place where God had effected an atonement and propitiation required by God himself in order to be able to grant forgiveness, cleansing, and reconciliation to mortals like Isaiah.

This live coal touched Isaiah's mouth, preparing God's messenger to speak on behalf of the government of heaven. The effect and power of Isaiah's sin were broken. It is not as if there was something inherent in the live coal itself, but the *sign* must be linked with the *truth* if we are to understand what happened here. Accordingly, when sin and iniquity are taken away, the experience can be a scorching one indeed.

The prophet had little if anything to do with the "touching" and "taking away," for God was the initiator and the one who worked it all out. Isaiah only confessed with his lips, but God dealt with his iniquity. He alone "atoned" for Isaiah's sin (v. 7). The word "atoned" is the Hebrew word *kipper*, which means "to ransom or to deliver by means of a substitute." God himself was the one who paid the "ransom price," effecting the deliverance for the prophet just as it does for all of God's men and women who accept him and his work on the cross for us.

II. By Our Responding to God's Call (Isa. 6:8–10)

A. *God Issues His Call.* Finally, after Isaiah witnesses such a majestic scene with so many sensory effects, the Lord himself speaks in verse 8. There is no coercion put on the prophet, nor is he directly addressed, surprisingly enough. God simply wants to know, "Whom shall I send? And who will go for us?" The "us" here, as in several Old Testament passages, is the plural of majesty or royalty. Indeed, the New Testament relates the passage that follows directly to our Lord Jesus himself in John 12:41.

B. *God Hears the Response to His Summons.* Isaiah responds immediately, "Here am I. Send me!" (v. 8). He does not argue with God as Moses did, nor does he ask for further signs as Gideon did. He is more than ready; one steady, long look at the majesty of God, and it is more than an honor to do whatever God wants him to do.

C. *God Announces His Message to His Messenger.* All too many sermons and lessons based on this chapter in Isaiah end with verse 8, for many are bewildered or offended by the message that the prophet was given. Apparently some feel exactly the way that Isaiah's contemporaries felt, that he taught with the simplicity and bluntness of an unsophisticated country bumpkin, for in Isaiah 28:9–10 the drunken revelers mocked the straightforwardness of his teaching as if he were a little schoolboy rattling off his alphabet, or some pedant insisting that everyone dot their i's and cross their t's. To them it sounded similar to how "mind your p's and q's" sounds to us. The Hebrew behind the NIV rendering of Isaiah 28:10, "Do and do, do and do, rule on rule, rule on rule," is *tsaw latsaw, tsaw latsaw, qaw laqaw, qaw laqaw.* The two Hebrew letters *tsade* and *qoph* stand side by side in the Hebrew alphabet about where our *p* and *q* come in the English alphabet. So it must be read in a cynical or a mocking way that makes fun of the prophet for being so plain and straightforward in all that he was teaching and preaching.

It is clear that Isaiah's message was not intended to bring actual physical blindness to his listeners, but if the people were resistant to the message, then Isaiah was to keep on repeating the same words to them, even though this exposed his listeners to the possibility of rejecting the truth so frequently that they no longer would even hear what was being said because their hearts had been hardened. The prophet was to speak to "this people" (v. 9) the Lord's message. No longer are they designated as "my people." Heretofore, such a strong expression for hearing (the Hebrew is literally "hear a hearing," v. 9) usually connoted both an acknowledgment of what had been said and an implicit understanding that what was heard also would be done. Not in this instance, however. In the same way "see a seeing" did not imply that what was seen was acted upon by those who were ministered to any more than what was heard was put into action. If one notes the numerous times this text is cited in the New Testament, one will also notice that half of those times the emphasis is on divine sovereignty and the other times it is on human responsibility. For some, whose hearts were hard, the hearing and seeing only pushed them further into their state of belligerence and refusal to repent. But for those whose hearts were soft and tender toward God, the same preaching and teaching had the opposite effect, just as the sun has different effects on the material it hits—melting wax but hardening concrete.

D. *God Describes the Task of His Messenger.* Given the present set of circumstances in Judah, Isaiah's preaching would not make it easier for the people to repent and believe. Instead, his teaching would make it more difficult as ears, eyes, and hearts would grow duller and duller with gross apathy.

Even though Isaiah knew that his preaching was not going to have a lot of positive results, nevertheless he was to continue on. He was not to alter his message or pull his punches; the truth of God was the only remedy that could bring healing to the people. Yet that was what the people would hate and reject. So despite the dreary outcomes envisioned, the prophet's task was to bring a fresh word from God and to give it as faithfully as he could, regardless of the results.

III. By Our Responding to God's Purpose (Isa. 6:11–13)

A. *There Will Be a Time Limit.* Naturally, the prophet wanted to know "For how long, O LORD?" (v. 11). How long should he continue and expect the opposite results that most teachers and preachers hope and expect will result from their ministries? Is this just a short-term thing, or will it go into the future for a good while to come? One cannot help but hear a note of dismay in this question. Is it not possible, one would think, that after a while many would catch on and a gentle turnaround could be expected from his audiences? Isaiah does not resign, nor does he demand that God explain himself. Isaiah had promised God that he would go; that was his part of the deal. He will go, then, as he has been sent, but he goes with a heavy heart.

B. *There Will Be Desolation and Desertion of the Land and Cities.* Indeed, because of the adamant disobedience, the cities will be emptied and the land will lie desolate. The people will be deported, and the land will appear forsaken and empty due to the people's intransigence and refusal to heed the word from a holy God.

It was known by then that the policy of Assyria was to deport part of the population and to import other conquered peoples, creating a cacophony of languages and peoples with little or no chance of understanding each other.

Only a "tenth" will remain (v. 13), as if they were a leftover tithe that the land had failed to offer to God, the "tenth" that Leviticus 27:32–33 had ordered to be holy to the Lord. But even that "tenth" is vulnerable, for the land will be totally laid waste.

God's holiness also has some corollaries that many may find surprising. Included in the holiness of God are his jealousy and wrath.[11] *Jealousy* is a biblical word that is different from our own word as applied to mortals. It is not that God has envy, as mortals usually mean when they use this word; but there is a proper divine jealousy that brooks no rival. Deuteronomy 6:14–15 teaches: "Do not follow other gods, the gods of the peoples around you; for the LORD your God, who is among you, is a jealous God and his anger will burn against you, and he will destroy you from the face of the land." Joshua also reminded his people, "You are not able to serve the LORD. He is a holy God; he is a jealous God" (Josh. 24:19).

So we must fairly teach that aspect of the holiness of God that exhibits the fierceness of his holiness, which is so often foreign to our own way of thinking. Accordingly, when Uzzah, who was one

of the Levitical line and therefore should have known better, put
the ark of God on a cart, contrary to God's instructions, and then
reached out to touch that which was holy and set apart to God, he
was quickly punished (2 Sam. 6:6–7). Yet the Philistines, who had
not been taught about the sanctity of the ark of God, freely touched
it with no adverse consequences (1 Sam. 5–6). The outcry of the
Israelites to God's judgment on the people of Beth Shemesh, who
gawked on the sacred ark of God resulting in the death of many,
was unjustified. They cried, "Who can stand in the presence of the
LORD, this holy God?" (1 Sam. 6:20).

These were cases of wrongful infringements on what had been
separated from the times (i.e., what was "holy" and set apart to
God from all that was "secular," which means "of the times"). The
moral purity of God demands moral exactness from those who
would have any dealings with God or live in the world he has made.
God's holiness is not simply his exclusive "otherness"; it is also his
perfect moral purity, which sets the standard toward which we
must all strive.

C. *There Will Be a Seed of Holiness out of the Stump.* Just as the
oak and terebinth trees are felled and only stumps remain for the
most part, so in this situation the scene presents a similar type of
desolation.

However, amazingly, out of a stump in the midst of all this up-
heaval and mass destruction there arises a "holy seed" (v. 13). A
whole new start is found in this scene of chaos. But this allusion to
a stump prepares us for and makes us think of Isaiah 11:1, which
speaks of the "shoot" that arises out of the "stump of Jesse." Surely
this is a messianic allusion.

Thus, the hope for the future is the promise of the Messiah out
of the line of Jesse and David. But the prophet also used the col-
lective singular, "seed," which typically refers to the one (the Lord
Jesus) and the many (all who believe in every age). Thus the people
will finally enjoy the ancient promise-plan of God—the promise
made to Eve, Shem, Abraham, Isaac, Jacob, David, Solomon, and
the others in that line. The many of this "seed" are the remnant who
will believe and who have heard, seen, and acted on what they have
heard and seen.

Conclusions

1. The holiness of God, which speaks of his transcendence and separateness from all sin and this world, calls forth from all of us a life that is separate and different from the culture and the ethos of our day. He must not be trivialized or treated as if he were ordinary or common in any sense of the term.

2. The holiness of God elicits from his people a ready response of "Here am I, send me." God is still looking for a few good men and women who are not afraid of laying their all on the line for whatever aspect of service he calls them to. This is not an exclusive feature for those who are called into full-time work, but for all of God's followers.

3. The holiness of God must lead naturally into our joining the heavenly host in worship and song to the majesty, glory, and distinctiveness of our God. How can we resist expressing our song and worship to the one who is altogether different and set apart from all else?

4. Finally, the holiness of God is celebrated because out of his nature he sets up a norm for acting, thinking, and living that is very different and separate from the patterns of our times. We are called to live a life that uses his character as the basis and ground of all that we do and say. God's anger and wrath will fall on those who reject his holiness, not simply because they are imperfect, but because they have rejected his word and despised his standard as set forth in his character and life.

ENDNOTES

Introduction

1. John Piper, *The Supremacy of God in Preaching*, rev. ed. (Grand Rapids: Baker Books, 2004), 13.

2. Richard A. Muller, *Post-Reformation Reformed Dogmatics: The Rise and Development of Reformed Orthodoxy, ca. 1520 to ca. 1725*, vol. 3, *The Divine Essence and Attributes* (Grand Rapids: Baker Academic, 2003), 540.

3. See Exodus 33:18; Psalm 29:9; 1 Corinthians 13:12; 1 Timothy 6:16; and Hebrews 1:3.

4. Bryan Chapell, *Christ-Centered Preaching: Redeeming the Expository Sermon*, 2nd ed. (Grand Rapids: Baker Academic, 2005).

5. Sidney Greidanus, *Preaching Christ from the Old Testament* (Grand Rapids: Eerdmans, 1999).

6. Calvin Miller, *Preaching: The Art of Narrative Exposition* (Grand Rapids: Baker Books, 2006), 62–65.

7. Chapell, *Christ-Centered Preaching*, 281–88.

8. Greidanus, *Preaching Christ from the Old Testament*, 227–29.

9. Ibid., 228.

10. Ibid., 230.

11. Ibid., 232.

12. Christopher J. H. Wright, *Knowing Jesus Through the Old Testament: Rediscovering the Roots of Our Faith* (Downers Grove, IL: InterVarsity Press, 1992), 28.

13. Greidanus, *Preaching Christ from the Old Testament*, 233.

14. Walter C. Kaiser Jr., *Toward an Old Testament Theology* (Grand Rapids: Zondervan, 1978), and Kaiser, *The Christian and the "Old" Testament* (Pasadena, CA: William Carey Library, 1998).

15. See David L. Allen's great essay entitled "A Tale of Two Roads: The New Homiletic and Biblical Authority," *Preaching* 18 (2002): 27–38. Allen suggests on page 31 that "The birth of the New Homiletic occurred in 1971 when Craddock's *As One Without Authority: Essays on Inductive Preaching* was published. He initiated a move away from the so-called 'deductive, propositional' approach to a more inductive concept." Allen goes on to describe how David Buttrick and others continued this shift, especially in Buttrick's book *Homiletic: Moves and Structures* (Philadelphia: Fortress, 1987). Allen sees two foundational tenets to the New Homiletic (p. 32): (1) Discursive, deductive, and propositional preaching is no longer viable, and (2) the goal of preaching is not the communication of information (which is secondary or even tertiary at best), but instead it is the evocation of an experience in which the audience, with the help of the preacher, is led to create and discover new meanings of their own.

16. Haddon Robinson, foreword, to *Preaching the Old Testament*, ed. Scott M. Gibson (Grand Rapids: Baker Books, forthcoming), 8–9.

17. See Terence P. McGonigal, "Every Scripture is Inspired: An Exegesis of II Timothy 3:16–17," *Studia Biblica et Theologica* 3 (1978): 53–64. Also see Walter C. Kaiser Jr., *Toward Rediscovering the Old Testament* (Grand Rapids: Zondervan, 1987), 26–32, and Kaiser, "A Neglected Text in Bibliology Discussions: I Corinthians 2:6–16," *Westminster Theological Journal* 38 (1981): 307–10.

Chapter 1: Magnifying the Incomparability of Our God

1. See Walter C. Kaiser Jr., "Hermeneutics and the Theological Task," *Trinity Journal* 12 (1991): 3–14, and Kaiser, *Toward an Exegetical Theology* (Grand Rapids: Baker Academic, 1981): 131–47, "Theological Analysis."

Chapter 2: Magnifying the Greatness of Our God

1. Herodotus, *Histories*, I, 178–87.

2. James Pritchard, *Ancient Near Eastern Texts*, 3rd ed. (Princeton: Princeton University Press, 1969), 308.

Chapter 4: Magnifying the Wonderful Name of Our God

1. I am beholden for many of the ideas in this section to Allen P. Ross and his article on "Shem" in *The New International Dictionary of Old Testa-*

ment Theology and Exegesis, ed. Willem A. VanGemeren (Grand Rapids: Zondervan, 1997), 4:147–51.

2. See the photograph of this stamp seal in David Tarler, "Bullae from the City of David: A Hoard of Seal Impressions from the Israelite Period," *Biblical Archaeologist* 49 (1986): 204.

Chapter 5: Magnifying the Pardoning Grace of Our God

1. See Allen P. Ross, "The Biblical Method of Salvation: A Case for Discontinuity," in *Continuity and Discontinuity*, ed. John S. Feinberg (Westchester, IL: Crossway Books, 1988), 175; See "kaparu," in *The Assyrian Dictionary of the Oriental Institute of the University of Chicago*, ed. A. Leo Oppenheim (Chicago: Oriental Institute, 1978), 8:178.

2. See T. V. Farris, *Mighty to Save: A Study in Old Testament Soteriology* (Nashville, TN: Broadman Press, 1993), 146, 149.

3. R. Laird Harris, "kipper," in *Theological Wordbook of the Old Testament*, ed. R. Laird Harris, Gleason L. Archer Jr., and Bruce K. Waltke (Chicago: Moody, 1981), 1:453. Also, Walter C. Kaiser Jr., "Salvation in the Old Testament: With Special Emphasis on the Object and Content of Personal Belief," *Jian Dao: A Journal of Bible and Theology*, Issue 2 (1994): 1–18.

4. See Hobart Freeman, "The Problem of Efficacy of Old Testament Sacrifices," *Bulletin of the Evangelical Theological Society* 5 (1962): 73–79. Also, Ralph H. Elliott, "Atonement in the Old Testament," *Review and Expositor* 59 (1962): 1–15.

5. Vincent Taylor, *The Atonement in New Testament Teaching*, 2nd ed. (London: Epworth, 1945), 177n2.

6. See A. M. Stibbs, *The Meaning of the Word 'Blood' in Scripture* (London: Tyndale, 1948), 3–32.

7. C. F. Keil and F. Delitzsch, *Biblical Commentary of the Old Testament: The Twelve Minor Prophets*, trans. James Martin (Grand Rapids: Eerdmans, 1954), 1:510.

8. As cited by C. F. Keil, ibid., 1:510.

9. Paul Kleinert, "Micah" in ed. Johann Peter Lange, *A Commentary on the Holy Scriptures: Critical, Doctrinal and Homiletical with Special References to Ministers and Students*. Trans. and ed. Phillip Schaff (New York: Scribner, 1874; repr., Grand Rapids: Zondervan, 1957).

10. For a fuller treatment of this idea, see the explanation in chapter 7 later in this work.

Chapter 6: Magnifying the Holy Spirit from Our God

1. Herman Hanko, "Charles Grandison Finney: Revivalist (3)," *The Standard Bearer* 82, no. 13 (March 15, 2006): 283.

2. Walter C. Kaiser Jr., *Revive Us Again: Biblical Insights for Encouraging Spiritual Renewal* (Nashville, TN: Broadman and Holman, 1999).

3. T. Goodwin, *Works* (Edinburgh: T & T Clark, 1961), V:8. Quoted in G. Smeaton, *The Doctrine of the Holy Spirit* (London, 1958), 49.

4. Smeaton, *Doctrine*, 49.

5. A. B. Simpson, *The Holy Spirit* (Harrisburg: Christian Publications, n.d.), I:137.

6. This observation was made in a major paper by my ThM student YunGab Choi in the fall of 2005.

7. For further development of this basic thesis, see John Rea, "The Personal Relationship of Old Testament Believers to the Holy Spirit," in *Essays on Apostolic Themes: Studies in Honor of Howard M. Ervin*, ed. Paul Elbert (Peabody, MA: Hendrickson Publishers, 1985), 92–103; Gary Fredricks, "Rethinking the Role of the Holy Spirit in the Lives of Old Testament Believers," *Trinity Journal* 9 (1988), 81–104; John Goldingay, "Was the Holy Spirit Active in Old Testament Times? What Was New About the Christian Experience of God?" *Ex Auditu* 12 (1996), 14–28; Geoffrey W. Grogan, "The Experience of Salvation in the Old and New Testament," *Vox Evangelica* 5 (1967), 4–26.

8. Not as the NIV and the NASB have it in the future tense translation. However, these are clearly *waw* conversives with imperfect Hebrew tense, which is routinely rendered as the narrative past tense.

9. I am beholden to David Baron, along with numerous other commentators, for his help on this passage. Baron's work is *Commentary on Zechariah: His Visions and Prophecies* (Grand Rapids: Kregel, 1988).

Chapter 7: Magnifying the Awesome Character of Our God

1. For help in this section on God's omniscience, I am beholden to my former colleague John S. Feinberg and his work *No One Like Him: The Doctrine of God* (Wheaton, IL: Crossway Books, 2001), 299–320.

2. Again, I have been helped enormously by the discussion of John S. Feinberg, *No One Like Him*, 249–55.

3. Once again, I turn to John S. Feinberg for assistance on "omnipotence," in *No One Like Him*, 277–94.

4. Bruce A. Ware, in his book *God's Lesser Glory: The Diminished God of Open Theism* (Wheaton, IL: Crossway Books, 2000), 100n2, documents

the fact that Steve Roy, a doctoral student and faculty member at Trinity Evangelical Divinity School, conducted this research and reported these figures.

5. Reported by Donald Glenn in "An Exegetical and Theological Exposition of Psalm 139," in *Tradition and Testament: Essays in Honor of Charles Lee Feinberg*, ed. John S. Feinberg and Paul D. Feinberg (Chicago: Moody, 1981), 161.

Chapter 8: Magnifying the Glory of Our God

1. See C. John Collins, "kbd," in *The New International Dictionary of Old Testament Theology and Exegesis*, ed. Willem A. VanGemeren (Grand Rapids: Zondervan, 1997), 2:577–87.

2. Walter C. Kaiser Jr., *Toward an Old Testament Theology* (Grand Rapids: Zondervan, 1987), 120.

3. G. L. Bray, "Glory," in *New Dictionary of Biblical Theology*, ed. T. Desmond Alexander *et al.* (Downers Grove, IL: InterVarsity Press, 2000), 508.

4. Stuart Briscoe, *All Things Weird and Wonderful* (Wheaton, IL: Victor Books, 1977), 16.

5. Briscoe, *All Things Weird*, 16.

6. Lamar Eugene Cooper Sr., *Ezekiel*, The New American Commentary 17 (Nashville, TN: Broadman and Holman, 1994), 66.

7. Daniel I. Block, "The Prophet and the Spirit: The Use of *rwh* in Ezekiel," *Journal of the Evangelical Theological Society* 32 (1989): 28. Isaiah's book uses "spirit" 51 times, and Jeremiah only 18 times.

8. Ibid., 29, 34–36.

9. Daniel I. Block, *Ezekiel*, The New International Commentary on the Old Testament (Grand Rapids: Eerdmans, 1997), 1:103–4n95.

10. These thoughts are a summary of the section in Daniel I. Block's work (*Ezekiel*, 106–9) entitled "Theological Implications."

Chapter 9: Magnifying the Grace of Giving from Our God

1. I am beholden to Stephen Olford for many of the concepts that follow from his book *The Grace of Giving: Biblical Expositions* (Memphis, TN: Encounter Ministries, Inc., 1972).

2. Bruce Waltke, *The Book of Proverbs: Chapters 1–15* (Grand Rapids: Eerdmans, 2004), 103.

3. Lest it be thought that these amounts are impossible and simply exaggerated, see Walter C. Kaiser Jr., *A History of Israel: From the Bronze*

Age Through the Jewish Wars (Nashville, TN: Broadman and Holman, 1998), 280–82. Also see Alan R. Millard, "Does the Bible Exaggerate King Solomon's Golden Wealth?" *Biblical Archaeology Review* 15, no. 3 (1989), 21–29, 31, 34; and Kenneth A. Kitchen, "Where Did Solomon's Gold Go?" *Biblical Archaeology Review* 15, no. 3 (1989), 30.

4. M. G. Abegg Jr., "gdl," in *The New International Dictionary of Old Testament Theology and Exegesis*, ed. Willem A. VanGemeren (Grand Rapids: Zondervan, 1977), 1:825–27.

5. Robin Wakely, "gbr," in *The New International Dictionary of Old Testament Theology and Exegesis*, 1:812–14.

6. C. John Collins, "p'r," in *The New International Dictionary of Old Testament Theology and Exegesis*, 3:573–74.

7. C. John Collins, "hod," in *The New International Dictionary of Old Testament Theology and Exegesis*, 1:1016–17.

8. C. John Collins, "nsh," in *The New International Dictionary of Old Testament Theology and Exegesis*, 3:139–41.

Chapter 10: Magnifying the Holiness of Our God

1. Jackie A. Naude, "qdsh," in *The New International Dictionary of Old Testament Theology and Exegesis*, ed. Willem A. VanGemeren (Grand Rapids: Zondervan, 1997), 3:877.

2. If *holiness* is the closest synonym for God's transcendence in the Old Testament, a close second to *holy* is *glory*, a word that depicts the unapproachable majesty and brilliance of his person and presence, marking him out as "the King of Glory" (Ps. 24:7–10).

3. A. W. Tozer, *The Knowledge of the Holy: The Attributes of God: Their Meaning in the Christian Life* (San Francisco: Harper San Francisco, 1961), 103–4.

4. Rudolph Otto, *The Idea of the Holy*, trans. J. W. Harvey (New York: Oxford Press, 1958). The most thorough treatment of the concept of holiness in English is by John G. Gammie, *Holiness in Israel* (Philadelphia: Fortress, 1989).

5. Walter C. Kaiser Jr., "The Book of Leviticus," in *The New Interpreter's Bible* (Nashville, TN: Abingdon Press, 1994), 1:1132.

6. J. Alec Motyer. *The Prophecy of Isaiah: An Introduction and Commentary* (Downers Grove, IL: InterVarsity Press, 1993), 77n1.

7. H. H. Rowley, *The Faith of Israel* (London: SCM, 1956), 66; cited in ibid., 77n3.

8. Motyer, *The Prophecy of Isaiah*, 75.

9. Others, such as E. Thiele, placed Uzziah's death in 739 BC and a few as late as 735 BC, but none of these approximate dates affect the meaning of the message here.

10. Motyer, *The Prophecy of Isaiah*, 76. John N. Oswalt, *The Book of Isaiah, Chapters 1–39* (The New International Commentary on the Old Testament; Grand Rapids: Eerdmans, 1986), 178, also adds Isaiah 52:13 as another example of this pair of words, there rendered in the NIV as "he will be raised and lifted up."

11. I am beholden to R. T. France for his analysis of this aspect of God's holiness in his book *The Living God: A Personal Look at What the Bible Says about God* (Downers Grove, IL: InterVarsity Press, 1970), 64–66.

AUTHOR INDEX

.

.

.

.

.

.

.

.

.

.

SCRIPTURE INDEX

Subject Index

Subject Index

idolatry, 33
immensity of God, 108
inaugurated eschatology, 95
interest test, 19
interrogative, 13–14, 28, 56, 69, 84, 96, 112, 123, 136, 147

jealousy of God, 154
Jehoahaz, 109
Jehoiachin, 123
Jerusalem Bible, 101
Joshua, 97, 100

Kimchi, Rabbi, 101
Korah's men, 58

lampstand, 100, 103
Louis XIV, 42
love, definition of, 74

maiestas Dei, 12
majesty, 9
Massillon, 42
meaning, plurality of, 18
Melchizedek, 63, 132–33
Moses, 57–63, 120–21
mysterium tremendum, 145

name, theology of, 65–67, 120
Nebuchadnezzar, 37–41, 70, 123
new covenant, 76
new homiletic, 19
Nicodemus, 93

omnipotence, 105, 110–12, 117
omnipresence, 105, 108–10, 117
omniscience, 105, 106–8, 117
open theism, 112

pantokrator, 110
pardon, 88, 90
Pentecost, 92
pericope, 28
plagiarism, 54
pottery lamps, 98
preaching of the Old Testament, 20
promise-plan of God, 18
property redemption, 70–71
pseudepigraphal books, 45

redemptive-historical method, 16
restoration of Israel, 75
revival(s), 9, 92
Rockefeller, John D., 136
Rosh Hashanah, 89
rubric(s), 28, 110

salvation in the Old Testament, 79–84
Sarah, 73
sedes doctrine, 23
seraphim, 149
sermon, Christian, 14–19
sermon, Judaistic, 18
Serpent, the, 87
"servant, my," 98
seven churches, 100
Sheol, 114
shrine prostitutes, 150
significance(s), 17
summaries, 18
systematic theology, 105–6

Tashlich, 89
theonomists, 111
theophany, 52, 127, 129, 148–49
Tiglath-pileser III, 148
tithing, 133–36
Titus's Arch, 98
transcendence, 144
trisagion, 144, 149
Tyre, 43, 45–46

Uzzah, 154
Uzziah, 147–48, 151

Vanderbilt, W. H., 137

"watcher," 45
worship, 130

Yeltsin, Boris, 47
Yom Kippur, 80–83, 89

Zedekiah, 68, 74, 104
Zerubbabel, 100, 102